PRAISE FOR THE BOOK

❝ It's hard to find a reliable source of information about the differences between the various African Traditional Religions (ATRs). In the New World, all of the various traditions tend to get lumped under the umbrella term "Voodoo," making it hard for nonpractitioners to differentiate between them. In *Voodoo and African Traditional Religion,* Lilith Dorsey tackles this challenge by providing a brief look at the history and practices that make up the major ATRs and doing so with great finesse. From Yoruba, Haiti, and Brazil to New Orleans and beyond, Dorsey provides a nice introduction to these various traditions and religions. I highly recommend *Voodoo and African Traditional Religion* to anyone who wishes to learn the sacred stories and practices associated with the religions of our Ancestors."

Denise Alvarado, author of *The Magic of Marie Laveau* and *Witch Queens, Voodoo Spirits, and Hoodoo Saints: A Guide to Magical New Orleans*

❝ I was fortunate to run across an earlier iteration of this book a few years back and am delighted to see it expanded and republished. Lilith Dorsey's grasp of the differences and similarities of these many African traditions (as well as their American offspring) is much needed as these spiritualities and religions continue to attract new adherents. It is no secret that we are seeing a blossoming of what used to be termed "alternative spiritualities," but the ones whose roots are in Africa are especially beautiful and powerful—and not as well understood or respected as they should be. Lilith Dorsey's book will go a long way toward enlightening people who are seeking, as well as educating people (like me) who want to know more. A must-have for your religions and spirituality bookcase—you'll go back to it again and again."

H. Byron Ballard, Witch, folklorist, and author of *Staubs and Ditchwater, Seasons of a Magical Life,* and *Roots, Branches & Spirits: The Folkways & Witchery of Appalachia*

❝ Lilith Dorsey is one of the few sincere and informed scholar-practitioners who is able to synthesize an expansive knowledge of traditional spirituality into a readable narrative that incorporates history, instruction, and practical guidance for anyone wishing to learn more about African and African American religions and magic. With an updated film, recording, and reading list, the book is an excellent resource that addresses the current turn to ancient spiritual wisdom to confront some of our most pressing societal needs."

Yvonne Chireau, Professor of Religion at Swarthmore College and author of *Black Magic: Religion and the African American Conjuring Tradition*

❝ Lilith Dorsey's second edition of *Voodoo and African Traditional Religion* is a milestone for the correct information on Africa and their diasporic religions. Too often misunderstood and ostracized, the religions of the African diaspora create bridges and are examples of tolerance, problem-solving, peace, and cooperation between different cultures, nations, beliefs, and lifestyles. Lilith Dorsey is a well-known and respected Priestess and Leader and gives us a simple but deep approach for the reader on the fastest growing underground Religions of modern times. There's a light in this book that will guide people to a better approach and respect for legacies and differences: a correct understanding."

Manuel Congo, Global Ethnologist and author of *The Lucumi Tarot*

❝ It is not very often that books on African Diasporic spiritual and magical traditions keep my attention beyond the first couple of pages. So, imagine my delight and joy at finding myself devouring this book in one sitting. Lilith Dorsey restored my soul with the thoroughness of this work. Shadowing the travels of souls brought into these continents and islands with impeccable research, Lilith has brought us through centuries of survival and worship. Moving past the big three, Ifá, Santería, and Voodoo, the book takes us into even more spaces where African beliefs took other forms and formats. Including Hoodoo, with a true understanding of its juxtaposition with religion, brought a correct perspective to an often contentious topic.

Lilith's commitment to documentation, research, oral and written history sings through the pages. I felt like I was back in the library stacks, back when there were some. I could feel the pains and jubilations as Lilith painstakingly addressed the popular media's handling of these traditions for public consumption. The images evoked in the descriptions were full, rich, and meaningful. I envision this work as a mandatory read in college courses. *Voodoo and African Traditional Religion* feels like not only a labor of love but a divine order. I highly recommend both this book and its author."

Kenya T. Coviak, host of the Michigan Witches Ball and the Detroit Conjure and Folk Magic Festival

"Lilith Dorsey's *Voodoo and African Traditional Religion* guides us through the basics and common misconceptions of the African diaspora religions, from the Yoruba to the Candomblé, from explaining the divinities to the festivities calendar of each tradition. In this book, Lilith answered several of the curious questions I had about these religions but was too embarrassed to ask—especially the descriptions of the Orishas and Lwa and the clarifications about ceremonies and possessions. During these times of injustice and pain, this book's offering of the wisdom and history of these traditions may bring more than knowledge for those in need of resistance and protection."

Jaime Gironés, author *Llewellyn's Little Book of the Day of the Dead*, and columnist at The Wild Hunt

❝ Lilith Dorsey's *Voodoo and African Tradition Religion* provides a welcome overview of African spiritual practices. Lilith writes knowledgeably from the perspective of both a long-term scholar and from lived experience as a priestess. Dorsey carefully points out that each Vodou society practices differently and, with that in mind, offers principles, practices, formulas, ingredients, and simple rituals that allow those who are sincerely interested in getting their feet wet. It is always refreshing to discover a new resource that replaces misconceptions about these much-maligned and sensationalized religions with respectful information focused on the beautiful, life-affirming qualities of spiritual practices that have helped people find hope, healing, and survival. As always, thank you, Lilith Dorsey, for your dedicated Service and Work."

Manbo Asogwe Sallie Ann Glassman, co-creator of *The New Orleans Voodoo Tarot,* author of *Vodou Visions,* and co-founder of The New Orleans Healing Center

❝ Lilith Dorsey has given us a tremendous gift in their book *Voodoo and African Traditional Religion.* As a practitioner and anthropologist, Lilith communicates the sacred teachings of African traditional religions with one foot in the social sciences and one foot in sacred space. Their approach to introducing readers to the many diverse faiths of Africa is accurate, clear, and real. Lilith's passion for presenting traditions in a non-sensationalistic manner is clearly seen in their work as they describe the respect and consideration they have—and we all should have, for these living traditions."

Tony Kail, Anthropologist and Author of *A Secret History of Memphis Hoodoo: Rootwork, Conjure and Spirituals*

❝ For years the very few books on African traditions and Caribbean religions have been written by outsiders of these religions—treated like an exotic product and taken from people of color to be exploited and consumed by the general public. Rarely do we find a book on the subject written from the perspective and experience of a true practitioner. Finally, *Voodoo and African Traditional Religion* provides one of the few books on African spiritual and magical practices written by a woman of color with years of experience and international recognition within the field. Lilith Dorsey explains everything you need to know about the traditions of the African diaspora. You will understand the stories behind the Orixa, the Loa, and the Spirits associated with the Ifá, Yoruba, Vodou, Candomblé, Voodoo, and Hoodoo traditions and discover the history and culture behind these paths. The book culminates in a magickal manifesto of black spiritual liberation, including techniques for protection and protest in the modern age, where people of color continue to face challenges simply due to the color of their skin. *Voodoo and African Traditional Religion* is a true compilation of black culture and black religion—written by a black woman."

Elhoim Leafar, Author of *The Magical Art of Crafting Charm Bags*, and *Manifestation Magic*

No one makes New Orleans Voodoo more accessible and approachable than Lilith Dorsey. Do you have questions about Vodou, Santeria, and Hoodoo? This book is the best place to start. A must-have book for the library of every well-read magickal practitioner."

Jason Mankey, High Priest, Initiate, and author of *Transformative Witchcraft: The Greater Mysteries*

Groundbreaking...Engages the head with extensive accounts of the diasporic African religions, the hands with useful, practical descriptions of their magic and spellcraft, and the heart with wise advice."

Louis Martinié, co-author of *The New Orleans Voodoo Tarot*

An enlightening and immersive guide full of helpful information for both beginners and longtime practitioners. Lilith does a great job of presenting a wide variety of intriguing facts and experiences that are sure to capture the interest of any soul that is seeking on their spiritual journey."

Fatima Mbodj, author of the *New Orleans Oracle Deck* and proprietor of Path of Awakenings in New Orleans, Louisiana

❝ If you are looking to begin an in-depth study of African Traditional Religions (ATR) and diaspora, start here. Lilith Dorsey cuts through the superstitions and sensationalism that the white cultural lens has placed on these vast practices with accurate explanations of initiation, sacrifice, and spells. Lilith then sets up would-be students of ATR study for success by sharing their vast knowledge on where to go next for further study. Whether learning ATRs or unlearning media manipulation, I highly recommend this book."

Diana Rajchel, author of *Urban Magick: A Guide for the City Witch*

❝ *Voodoo and African Traditional Religion* is filled with insightful historical and archaeological information on Voodoo, Vodou, Hoodoo, and other African Traditional Religions. It offers information on the whole gamut of Deities, Orishas, the Lwa, Saints, and more, making this another must-have, go-to book. For those wanting to research—and possibly find out about working with—the systems covered, this book brings deep insights into its many offerings and includes many spells and rituals. Lilith also recognizes and highlights those who have paved the way for African spiritual practices. This book will undoubtedly be referred to as one of the most comprehensive titles on the topic, and I will certainly recommend it to my students."

Starr RavenHawk, Founder of WFT Academy of Pagan Studies & NYC Wiccan Family Temple and proprietor of CharmedByStarr.com

❝ The original incarnation of this book was a complex combination of survey, glossary, comparison and was liberally sprinkled with Lilith Dorsey's view as an insider and practitioner. With this new edition, Dorsey's lens is much more provocative, feminist, and revolutionary. It retains the recipe book innocence of the original but is now closer to the Anarchist Cookbook than Betty Crocker. In introducing the reader to the various paths of the African diaspora, this book reveals the genius of the ancestors who escaped slavery and tried to make spiritual sense of a world that had stolen their culture, religion, and their very lives. Lilith's visceral and pragmatic view of the violence that has plagued Black Lives stands in this new edition—released at a time where the terrible legacy of slavery is at the forefront of the public consciousness, and the descendants of that legacy are rediscovering the spiritual tools of their ancestors. These tools offer new hope at a time when we would otherwise be helpless and hopeless. You don't have to read between the lines of this book to feel the inspiration that resurrected it makes it rise above a sea of misinformation and mythification that only someone who inhabits this world can truly share. Ese e Pupo, Iya Lilith."

Baba Teddy, author of *Absinthe, Alewives and Alchemy,* Oso of Iyami Osoronga, BabaL'awo Osun I'L'ode, Oluwo of Odu/Ifa, and Konchante of Gineh Yoruba VoDou

" Having collaborated and worked with Lilith Dorsey since 1999, I remember when the first edition of this book arrived in 2005. It was truly groundbreaking back then: a mainstream crossover from a Generation X black woman who was among the few you could count on one hand that was immersed in both the African Traditional Religions and the Neo-Pagan community—and an academic as well. Sixteen years later, this still holds true, Lilith Dorsey is still one of the very few black women to have become a prolific presenter across North America in both African Spiritual and Pagan communities as well as a best-selling author—a unique achievement for any person, and so Lilith truly stands alone.

In this newly revised update, *Voodoo and African Traditional Religion* will take its place once more among the integral books on the subject. This book will educate, inspire, and interact with the reader, and for many, it will lead them unto their destiny among the traditions. Lilith has gifted us with a truly sacred work that is an honor to all those who came before who maintained and preserved the Diasporic religions. The lineage continues."

Witchdoctor Utu, founder of the Dragon Ritual Drummers and author of *Conjuring Harriet "Mama Moses" Tubman and the Spirits of the Underground Railroad*

" Reading this book is like taking an immersion course in the rich history, culture, and spiritual offerings of traditional African religions. Lilith has not only crafted an informative and much-needed expert resource, dispelling misinformation and stigma around these sacred practices, she has also created a down-to-earth guidebook to empower readers in walking their own spiritual journey."

Mecca Woods, Astrologer and author of *Astrology for Happiness and Success* and *The Astrology Journal: A Celestial Guide to Recording Your Cosmic Journey*

AND AFRICAN TRADITIONAL RELIGION

Lilith Dorsey

Warlock Press™

VOODOO AND AFRICAN TRADITIONAL RELIGION
© 2021, Lilith Dorsey

Revised and expanded edition of *Voodoo and Afro-Caribbean Paganism* (Citidel Press, 2005)

All rights reserved. No part of this publication may be reproduced, stored in a retrieval system or transmitted in any form or by any means, electronic, mechanical, photocopying, recording or otherwise without the prior permission of the publisher or in accordance with the provisions of the Copyright, Designs and Patents Act 1988 or under the terms of any license permitting limited copying issued by the Copyright Licensing Agency.

Published by:
Warlock Press
1219 Decatur Street
New Orleans, 70116 LA, USA

Typesetting and Cover Design: Christian Day
Cover Photo and Author Photo: Carlos Fundora
Vévé Illustrations: Tehron Gillis
Interior Photos: Lilith Dorsey, Christian Bazan, Adobe Stock Photos, and public domain images.

ISBN-10: 1-7332466-3-7
ISBN-13: 978-1-7332466-3-7

ACKNOWLEDGEMENTS

Many thanks and much love to Nia Dorsey, Aria Dorsey, Priestess Miriam, Louis Martinié, Mishlen Linden, Utu and the Dragon Ritual Drummers, Gros Mambo Bonnie Devlin, Dr. Susan Johnson, Yeye Ochun Olukari Al'aye, Ogbe Di, Grace Buterbaugh, Alice Licato, Edith Licato, Prudy Dorsey, My Godchildren (Christian, Tehron, Vincent, Ziona, Dot, Tish, John, Jay, Glenn, Mel, Mark, Victoria, Tavia, Amanda, Iya Christina, Windafire, Bast, Rebeca Spirit), Indigo Ortiz, Emi, Baba Ian, Baba Walter, Sam Visnic, Ezra Visnic, Liam Nadeau, Phoenyx Precil, Scarlett Precil, Riva Nyri Precil, Clarivel Ruiz, Mina Bellavia, Cayne Micelli, Phat Man Dee, Cleomili Harris, Shaughn the Bard, Julio Jean, Jason Mankey, Lisi Tribble, Sen Elias, Christian Day, Brian Cain, Risa Sharpe, Spencer Adams, Jorge Lopez, Dustin Schneider, Mychael Scribner, Mary Cappello, Addison Smith, Faye Ginsburg, Cristina Esteras-Ortiz, Rachel True, Dorothy Morrison, Morganna Davies, Theitic, Diana L. Paxson, John Gray, Sunpie Barnes, Mac Rebennack, and all my honored ancestors.

CONTENTS

Acknowledgements XI
Preface to the New Edition XXII

Introduction 1

CHAPTER ONE
ROOTS OLD AND NEW — 12

The Orïsa 12
   Olodumare, Orunmilá, and Obatalá 13
   Eshú 13
   Sango 15
   Osün 16
   Oshosi 17
   Ogou 17
   Oyá and the Egungun 18
   Yemonja, Olokun, Nana Buruku 18
   Sonponno and Mami Wata 19
Sacred Art 20
Yoruba Calendar 21
Yoruban Sacred Stories 22
Yoruba Botanicals 23
Uncertain Future 24

CHAPTER TWO
HAITIAN VODOU — 25

Vodou History 26
The Lwa 26
   Legba 27
   Erzulie 28
   Damballa and Aida Wedo 29
   Marassa and Gran Bois 30
   Ayizan and Papa Loko 31
   Azaka and Gran Ibo 31

    Bossou, ShiLiBo, and Blanc Dani 32
    LaSirene 33
    Masa and Simbi 33
    Barons and Gede: The Ancestors 34
    Agwé 35
    Ogou 36
Spirit Marriage 36
Political History 38
Vodou Art 38
Vodou Drumming and Dance 41
Vodou Trance-Possession 44
The Feast of the Yam 44
Vodou Magickal Items 45
Vodou Calendar 46
Vodou Words of the Wise 46
Vodou Botanicals 47
Vodou Beyond the Seas 48

CHAPTER THREE
NEW ORLEANS VOODOO AND HOODOO   49
The Lwa 52
    Papa Lebat 52
    Annie Christmas 52
    Ogou 52
    LaSirene 53
    Mami Water 53
    Ayizan 53
    Madame LaLune 54
    Damballa and Aida Wedo 54
    Oshún and Erzulie 55
    The Ancestors 55
Hoodoo 56
The Saints Come Marching In 58
    Saint Peter 59
    Saint Anthony 59
    Saint Raymond 59
    Saint Joseph 59
    Saint Expedite 59

    Saint Rita 59
    Saint Marta 60
    Saint Dymphna 60
    Mary Magdalene 60
    Saint Martin DePorres 60
    Our Lady of Prompt Succor 60
    Saint Anne 60
    Saint Paul 60
Divination 61
The Art 61
The Music 61
The Magickal Items 63
The Calendar 64
The Mythology 65
The Botanicals 66
Extend Yourself 67

CHAPTER FOUR
SANTERÍA   69

Orisha 69
    Olorun 69
    Elegguá 70
    Ogún 71
    Ochosi 72
    Obatalá 73
    Orunmilá 74
    Yemaya 74
    Oshún 75
    Changó 76
    Aganyú 77
    Oyá 77
    Obá 78
    Babaluaiye and Nana Buluku 79
    Ibeji 79
    Osanyin 79
    Inle 80
Santería Drumming and Dance 80
Santería Initiations 81

Divination 83
Palo Monte or Palo Mayombe 84
Santería Calendar 85
Patakis 86
Santería Botanicals and Stones 87
Persecution and Prosecution 88

CHAPTER FIVE
SHANGÓ AND OBEAH 90

Shangó and Orisha 90
   Ogun 90
   Osain and Aireelay 91
   Shangó 91
   Aba Lofa 91
   Omira 91
   Mama Latay 91
   Ebejee 92
   Da Lua and Da Logee 92
   Yemanja 92
Obeah Traditions 92
   Myalism 93
   Duppies 93
Sacred Art of Trinidad and Belize 94
Shangó and Obeah Calendar 94
Jamaican Folklore 95
Obeah Herbs 96
Futures and Fighting 97

CHAPTER SIX
AFRICAN TRADITIONAL RELIGION IN BRAZIL 98

Candomblé 98
   Exú: The Devil at the Crossroads 100
   Pomba Gira: Sacred Sensuality 100
   Ogum: The Military General 102
   Oxum: A Vision of Love 103
   Oxala and Ossain: Sky and Earth 103
   Iemanja: Sea and Stars 103

Omolu: Sickness and Health. 103
Spiritism 103
Umbanda and Quimbanda 105
Afro-Brazilian Music and Dance 106
A Myth of Brazil 107
Calendar of Brazil 107
Botanicals of Brazil. 108
A Religion Comes to Life 108

CHAPTER SEVEN
SHRINES OF AFRICA AND BEYOND   110

Altars and Shrines 110
   Shrines of the Ifá faith 111
   Sacred Shrines of Vodou 111
   Voodoo Shrines of New Orleans 112
   The Shrines of Santería. 113
   Shrines in Trinidad 114
   Brazil: Shrines in the Land of the Living Statues 115
Create an Ancestor Shrine. 117
   A Note for the Adopted 118

CHAPTER EIGHT
VOODOO AND LUCUMÍ MAGICKAL WORKINGS   119

Ritual Cleansing and Baths 119
To Remove Unwanted Influences. 120
Véve Magick. 121
Ritual Feasts. 122
Candle Spells. 123
Voodoo Dolls 125
Gris-Gris 125
Magickal Oils 126
Divination. 129

CHAPTER NINE
VOODOO AND LUCUMÍ RELIGIOUS RITUALS   130

Ritual Practices 130
Group Ritual. 131

  Order of Service for Public Group Ritual 133
  Order of Service for Private Group Ritual 134
Solitary Ritual 135
  Creating a Magickal Journal 136
  A Ritual of Transformation 137

CHAPTER TEN
VOODOO ON THE SILVER SCREEN   138
Roll Credits 152

CHAPTER ELEVEN
BLACK ROOTS TO LIVE BY   153
Spells for Protection and Protest. 154
Recipes for Revolution 162
Nia and Umoja 165
Plant Roots, Harvest Food. 167

CHAPTER TWELVE
VOODOO GOLD AT THE RAINBOW'S END   169

APPENDIX ONE
Recommended Reading and Recordings 173

APPENDIX TWO
Resources for African Traditional Religion 185

APPENDIX THREE
Glossary of Terms 190
Index **198**

About the Author .207

PREFACE TO THE NEW EDITION

It has been almost two decades since I wrote the first edition of this book. Over these years, I've lost godparents, mentors, and friends, and gained godchildren and students in turn. It makes my heart heavy with both sadness and joy. The cycle of destiny moves through life, and sometimes the rebirth ushers in a whole new era. Don't get me wrong, Voodoo and the other African Traditional Religions are ancient, yet they artfully equip us for a new tomorrow.

Unfortunately, hurt and hardship are nothing new for African Traditional Religions; they were born of struggle. Built on the backs of Black people, they gained immeasurable strength and startling capacity for resolve. When I grew up, the bulk of these traditions were carried out in secrecy. Practitioners were vilified, ridiculed, and suffered other severe consequences at the hands of dominant oppressors. Fortunately, that has changed. Musicians, Artists, Activists, and Authors like myself have been able to publicly embrace these practices, sharing their beauty and bounty.

The words you find within these pages have been updated to reflect the world we face now. New challenges and new rewards unfold at every turn. Even in the past year, I've seen a reawakening within the religions, which people say have filled them with the knowledge to empower themselves on every level. May these words reawaken you! Ashé!

INTRODUCTION
A TIME TO TALK

As a longtime scholar and practitioner of Voodoo, Vodou, Santería, Candomblé, and even occasionally Palo Mayombe, I have long recognized the need for a book like this one. The African Diasporic religious traditions are both strikingly similar and vastly different. Dependent on a number of factors, the traditional mainstays from West African practice make up the sacred tapestry of these religions. This book gives a cursory examination of each of these traditions, the most common dos and don'ts in the religions, eventually leading up to rituals and offerings you can perform yourself. Hopefully, it will provide you with a springboard for further spiritual and academic study. You could spend the rest of your life just trying to fully comprehend even one small aspect of these ancient traditions. To that end, I have included at the close of this book a short description of recommended books and music relating to them.

It is also to be remembered that each temple, house, *ile*, or *hounfor* has its own specific set of rules and practices. One may offer a certain Orisha (Santería divinity; this is the most common spelling, mainly used in Cuba and Puerto Rico) one type of food in one area and the exact opposite in another. So if you are provided with information in these pages that goes against what you may have been taught, please follow the teachings you were given. I offer this information only as a guide for those wishing to explore some of the basic tenets of these divine systems of life and thought. In my graduate work with film, television studies, and anthropology at New York University, I did a lot of theorizing about meaning and truth. Ultimately, anyone living in our odd postmodern universe realizes that he or she has to discover his or her own beliefs based on a variety of factors such as culture and environment. This book stands as a survey of meaning and veracity in a set of religious worlds where secrets are often best kept secret, and meaning is almost always oral and ethereal.

One basic tenet of these religions is that every being and object is imbued with its own *ashé*. Ashé (pronounced *ah-shay* or *ah-say*) is a complex concept to understand; it operates like a universal life-force energy permeating all things. It is a divine current that means life, grace, blood, kingship, growth, power, force, and energy. It represents the essence of something, its being, and its intrinsic power. Everything contains its own ashé: people, gods, animals, places, trees, sounds, and even rocks. Ashé stands in opposition to chaos and disorder; it is the supreme being as a sacred power. Ashé is the ultimate absolute that defies definition.

In Voodoo and Santería, training is only based in part on factual knowledge, with the bulk of the learning concerning experiential and devotional knowledge. The teacher-student relationship is like a lifelong parent-child bond for followers of Voodoo and Santería.

FINDING A SPIRITUAL TEACHER

It would be wonderful if there were an easy set of rules that people could follow to determine the validity of one spiritual practice and practitioner or another, but that is just not the case. The truth of the matter is that practices and practitioners completely run the gamut.

Fortunately, most of the African Traditional Religions (ATRs) have their own internal ranking system based on lineage. Each spiritual family is judged on the reputation of its members. The drawback to this system is, obviously, that a person must be familiar with someone in the practices to research someone's background and reputation.

When two Lucumí or Santería initiates meet, one of the first things that they do is exchange lineages. Many times in certain cities of the United States, like New York and Miami, common spiritual ties are discovered. It is like finding a long-lost relative or discovering that you know someone's brother or sister. The people of the African Diaspora were forcibly scattered across the globe. This utilization of what anthropologists term *fictive kin*, or creating family relationships where blood ties do not exist, provides individuals with a strong support structure to replace conventional family bonds that were unfortunately destroyed. Some people think that you can judge a practitioner's validity—meaning his or her ability to teach you and confer the proper initiations—by who is charging the lowest price. Trust me, bargain shopping for initiations is not always a preferred method where your spiritual growth is concerned. In fact, it is highly discouraged. An expensive store is often thought to be more exclusive, so why shouldn't an expensive spiritual initiation be afforded the same prestige? One practitioner explained it to me thusly: Traditionally, in Nigeria a person was required to give long-term service to his or her priestess, priest, and spiritual house. This frequently required moving to the location of the temple and remaining there for a year or longer. When this traditional tribute is considered, the substitution of money in lieu of time makes much more sense in the modern world. Often, the money required for these ceremonies is used to pay for food, alcohol, flowers, clothing, herbs, candles, incense, offerings, and payment to the drummers and additional priests and priestesses to complete the tasks at hand.

Legba Grafitti. – [Photo by author]

As I have mentioned, once an individual goes through the process of initiation with an ile, he or she becomes part of the spiritual family and is expected to provide not only monetary support but also help with cooking, cleaning, herbal preparations, and the other daily tasks. Ultimately, I believe one should have the utmost faith in one's spiritual leaders. If you doubt them, you will eventually end up doubting yourself. I was at a *bembe* (Lucumí drum ceremony) once where someone became possessed by Oshún (the goddess of love and dance), who was quite taken with one of the young men there. She told him he possessed a great musical talent and he was just wasting it at his current job. Instead of following her advice, he took it as an insult to his chosen life. He did not quit his job, and he missed out on the special advice and blessings Oshún was trying to bestow on him. He is still struggling almost 20 years after these events occurred. Your spiritual teachers should always be your trusted confidants, friends, and mentors. In many ways, it is like choosing a physician, because this person holds your spiritual life and health in his or her hands.

I belabor this point because, as a Voodoo and Santería practitioner, lecturer, and author, I constantly meet people who describe unpleasant experiences with one ATR house or another. Once you attach yourself to a group that you are not happy with, there is very little, if anything, you can do about it. Not only is your money gone, you can't recoup the spiritual energy you have invested. I have heard stories of people taking their ritual items and either giving them away or throwing them into the ocean. I've seen people lock them away in closets or basements and try to ignore them. This may seem like a way to sever or lessen your ties, but rarely have I seen it be successful. Most often, people just end up continuing their practices on a less-formal basis. So please choose wisely the first time. Pick someone you trust and respect, who also has the same moral and ethical ideas as you do.

BEFORE YOU BEGIN

The recent popularity of New Orleans Voodoo, Haitian Vodou, Lucumí (more commonly called Santería), and other African-derived religions has created a surge in practices that are not always properly respectful and appropriate for practitioners to engage in. Some of this may be due to ignorance. So, to that end, I hope to explain some of the more basic rules that people should abide by. Beginners to the ceremonies should approach every aspect of the practices with the utmost respect and devotional care.

Voodoo and Lucumí have been continually practiced for hundreds, if not thousands, of years. As a result of this, there are strictly codified guidelines that often differ from those in place for practitioners of other religions.

There Is No Self-Initiation

These living religions have been cultivated throughout history to provide the seeker of spiritual guidance the ability to interact with a teacher. Every situation, from birth to death and everything in between, involves a variety of components that must be considered and examined by trained spiritual professionals. Just as in life, one cannot give birth to oneself. I once discussed this with a Haitian Vodou practitioner who told me this tenet was explained to him through a story. He asked his teacher the question: "If one cannot initiate oneself, who was then responsible for the first initiation?" His teacher responded, "In the very beginning there was the ashé, or spiritual power and energy, of the Lwa (Voodoo gods and goddesses), and the knowledge needed to be given to humankind. The Lwa temporarily took corporeal form and performed the necessary ceremonial rites for that first dedicant. From then on, the humans were able to complete the training of others themselves." There are various different sayings in Ifá, Candomblé, and other African-based traditions that stress emphatically that one cannot get awo (sacred knowledge) or give ebo (sacred offerings) after reading a book. This book is merely here to supplement and inform on an intellectual basis. Please leave complex spiritual matters, like initiation, to trained professionals.

What Can You Do Right Now?

Until you are properly initiated, most devotees of the religion believe all you can do is leave offerings, like food or drink, to honor the divine. It is not respectful to ask for anything, perform any specifically directed spells, or petition any energies or entities. Without proper training, you are simply not ready yet. Even practitioners who have been devoted to the tradition for over 50 years would not view their practices as summoning a divinity. One would never implore a Lwa or Orisha to arrive; it is more like humbly praying for their blessings.

Forget What You've Heard

Sexual abandon, sticking pins in Voodoo dolls, and flesh-eating zombies have nothing to do with the real practice of these religions. Please don't think they do. And explain this to your friends!

There is Great Beauty and Sublime Power in Silence

To hear the messages from the Orisha, you have to listen quietly. Some people spend an entire lifetime trying to learn this lesson. There are several times when a practitioner of Vodou or Santería must remain in total stillness for several days or weeks. Everything happens in its own time and according to its own pace. People often contact me seeking a local teacher, but sometimes this isn't possible. For decades, I had to travel thousands of miles to visit my spiritual teachers in New Orleans and Florida. Journeys can take many forms.

Don't Argue with Your Spiritual Elders

I am not implying that they are infallible, but arguing is not the proper way to conduct yourself with your spiritual teachers. Reexamine the situation for yourself first and, if you still have problems, discuss them calmly with your elders and other members of your spiritual family.

Cleanliness Really Is Next to God- And Goddessliness

Do not dishonor the traditions by being sloppy in either body, mind, home, or soul. If your surroundings are dirty, then you will just attract the dirty type of energy that will disrupt your life.

If Something Sounds Like A Really Bad Idea, Don't Do It!

I received this answer early in my training when I inquired about how one could validate the messages one was receiving. Please remember this—it is some of the best advice you will ever receive. Also remember that initiations and teachings are in place to provide necessary clarity.

Priesthood Isn't for Everyone

Not everyone is destined to become a mambo (Vodou priestess) or babalawo (Ifá or Santería high priest). Be thankful, be humble, and be patient. I know of one Santera (Lucumí priestess) who will not initiate any of her students until they are beyond their desire for such knowledge. An increased amount of spiritual power always carries with it tremendous responsibilities, consequences, and dedication. Most ATR houses experience growth gradually. Practitioners must be seasoned veterans, often functioning as students for decades, before they are allowed to reach the more advanced levels or degrees of the religion. Each person's process is slightly different and is shaped by life experiences and frequent divination.

Possession is Nine-Tenths of Voodoo Law

Possession is one of the most misunderstood aspects of these religions. In reality, it is a rite and a blessing for both the possessed person and the community as a whole. Many people tell me they are afraid of the experience, which seems to me to be akin to saying you are afraid of winning the lottery because it might be too much success for you to handle. The Orisha or Lwa need to establish a symbiotic relationship with humans so they can communicate, as well as give and receive favors. For a long time, this fear confused me until a friend told me that people believe possession will be like the movie *The Exorcist*. The power of media never ceases to amaze me. Orisha or Lwa possession could not be further from this demonic cinematic fantasy. The only way I can describe my personal experience is that it feels as if you are speaking with a voice similar to, yet different from your own. It's like the Orisha are speaking up for you because you happen to be in a challenging situation. This situation could be that you will have the wonderful opportunity to meet the partner of your dreams, or that the person standing next to you has a communicable disease. Their knowledge is infinite. When they come to speak through possession, everyone would do well to listen.

Follow the Rules

The various forms of these religions, be they Santería, Voodoo, or any of the others, have strict rules and regulations. There are taboos dealing with food and sex. They must be followed by all initiated worshippers of the tradition. Sometimes, the Orisha or Lwa will put roadblocks in the way to see if the petitioner is strong enough to carry out the challenge of serving properly in this religion. Some even theorize that it is for this reason the possession experience involves falling to the ground, just to see if the person is able to get back up and face the work ahead. Do your best to not get discouraged on your spiritual journey or you will be thought of as unworthy.

There is No Need to Fear

If you live your life with responsibility and proper behavior, the Orisha or Lwa will put you in the proper place for you to be the most effective member of society and the spiritual community.

Be Mindful in Your Approach

Each experience in your life should be approached with the greatest sense of compassion and an open heart of charity. Consider every situation from all perspectives: The rich man of today may be the pauper of tomorrow, and vice versa.

Practice Humility

Humility is also important to practitioners of these religions. During ceremonies, try to remain quiet unless prompted to do otherwise by spiritual forces or by a ritual participant. Please empathize with the fact that the ritual family or temple is trying to honor a large number of energies and entities.

Listen Deeply

Almost all, if not all, ceremonies will include times where the priest or priestess speaks to those present. Many times these messages will seem cryptic and confusing. There are a few reasons for this. First, many of the leaders of the African Diasporic community have speech patterns obviously rooted in the reality of African Diasporic culture. Blending of words, creolization, and multilayered meanings are all present in these forms. An additional reason for the complexity of the messages is that when the ancestors and the divine speak, it is not meant to be interpreted literally, but rather in the manner of a dream or oracle. The listener must be functioning on intuition and "feeling" the message.

POLYTHEISM
WE ALL HAVE A LOT OF GODS

Polytheism, or the belief in multiple divinities, is a tenet of New Orleans Voodoo, Haitian Vodou, Lucumí, and other religions. In a Judeo-Christian-dominated world, polytheism is definitely the minority belief system. When my father returned from the Million Man March in 1995, he said that there was a great unity among the Black men; different religions were embraced, as long as the religion "only had one god." The difference between the type of polytheism in the African Diasporic traditions and that of Judeo-Christian religions is one of hierarchy. Inherently, New Orleans Voodoo and the other ATRs have divinities that operate in a basically hierarchical structure. Most have a creator deity that is in many ways set apart from the other Orisha or Lwa. In Haitian Vodou, many see the deity whom they call Bon Dieu as being the same as the one of Christian monotheism.

The issue comes when we begin to look at the other honored figures in the religion. In Haitian Vodou and New Orleans Voodoo, these are most commonly known as Lwa, or Loa. Some see these operating as gods, others as similar to saints, and some see them as something else altogether.

GENDER ROLES
WOMEN ARE SMARTER—THAT'S RIGHT

Voodoo places a strong importance on the power of women. Many African Traditional Religions are oriented toward the divine feminine, allowing females a power over their own spirituality that is painfully lacking in traditional Christianity. In Voodoo temples, much of the power is held by women, which in part stems from the fact that during the time of slavery, the women were given the majority role in child-rearing and used it as an opportunity to educate young members of the community about their spiritual heritage.

In Voodoo, Santería (Lucumí), and the other African Diasporic religious traditions, there are always clearly defined gender roles. Many iles have strict taboos for menstruating women that limit their participation in group rituals during this time. For example, an initiate may be forbidden to touch others. This is an extreme level of devotion that, while it can be difficult, is meant to confer a specific set of blessings unique to the individual.

THINGS TO REMEMBER

A word about animal sacrifice: Many of the traditions profiled here involve the use of ritual sacrifice of animals. I believe the simplest way to explain it is with an analogy. I usually ask people: If your child or parent were diagnosed with a fatal illness and the only way to cure them was with medicine made from an animal source, would you refuse the treatment? No sacrifice is ever made lightly. They are performed as a necessity to protect and provide for the community by honoring the Orisha or Lwa.

Some thoughts about spelling: Many of these spiritual systems were orally transmitted and, consequently, there has been great variation in spelling and, to a lesser extent, in the pronunciation of the deities. Whenever possible, I have attempted to present all available spellings or permutations of the Orisha and Lwa explored in these pages.

Several people will also probably take issue with the fact that I choose to present several different traditions together in one volume. It is to be understood that I preserve strict boundaries between the variations of African Diasporic religious tradition. That said, the various forms of the religion, Candomblé, Voodoo, Shangó, Santería (Lucumí), Obeah, and others, still maintain basic patterns that are similar to each other and to a West African-derived set of thoughts and ritual practices. I do not believe that the Changó of Lucumí is the same as the Sangos, Shangós, and other deities with similar names—only that they share the same ashé. In this book, I will trace the differences between these religions as well as the similarities, providing a brief overview to these sacred traditions.

CHAPTER ONE

ROOTS OLD AND NEW
THE YORUBA CONNECTION

Many of the modern African-derived religious traditions stem from the region of West Africa. Arguably the most widely practiced form of the religion in existence today is the Yoruba religion most often referred to as *Ifá*. Ifá refers simultaneously to the religion, the divinity Ifá (Orunmilá), and the divination system that involves cowrie shells and a divining tray. The religion has several components in that it honors the Orïsa, practices ancestor worship, and uses divination.

The tradition of matriarchy and feminine power in the African Diasporic Religions is strong. Some even view the supreme creator divinity of the Yoruba, Olodumare, as a female. However, with goddesses like Yemonja, Oyá, Obá, Oshun, and others, the importance of women in the cosmology and the culture cannot be denied. Many of the systems are based on a balance between masculine fire, often catalyzed in the body of the drummers, and watery feminine receptivity, often embodied in the inspired dancers. These two forces work in conjunction to spiritually fertilize the universe and the congregation.

Ifá devotees believe the Orïsa to be the embodiment of ashé. Ogou, the lord of iron, is not a god who loves iron, but rather the ashé of iron. In Nigerian courts, witnesses are given the option of being sworn in with their hand touching a piece of iron. This is particularly interesting in a nation where most of the population identifies as either Christian or Muslim. Ashé is a power that can be felt, used, feared, and courted. The word is also used as an affirmation to mean "let it be" or "make it so."

THE ORÏSA

There are several deities present in the Yoruba pantheon. They are called Orïsa (Yoruba spelling of Orisha), and are, theoretically, primal energies, elevated ancestors, and individuals worthy of reverence after death. The Orïsa honored most often among the Yoruba in Nigeria today are Olodumare, considered by some the supreme being, then Orunmilá, Obatalá, Eshú, Ogou, Sonponno or Babaluaiye, Oshosi, Oshun, Yemonja, Oyá, Sango, Nana Buruku, Mami Wata, and Olokun.

Olodumare, Orunmilá, and Obatalá

The owner of both heaven and earth is called Olodumare, which translates very roughly to mean the Great One who continues without end. He or she, as the deity is sometimes represented, is also referred to as Oduduwa or Olorun. This divinity is to be welcomed as the highest of the gods in both the physical and spiritual realms.

Orunmilá is the Orïsa of divination. Believed to be a deputy of Olodumare in matters of omniscience, he is said to possess the mysteries about the very beginning of creation. Giving guidance and council to the community, Orunmilá is seen as the source of all Yoruba religious belief. Worshipped throughout the Yoruba territory, he is said to be a master linguist, speaking all languages. Orunmilá's knowledge is highly valued in the tradition, and he is said to have 16 *olodus*, or disciples, who assist him. Practitioners seek his guidance on a regular basis through divination. The shrine for Orunmilá is customarily placed in the home and is represented by a bowl with 16 palm kernels, cowries, and pieces of elephant tusk.

Obatalá is also seen as the gender-neutral creator divinity, representing the embodiment of clarity, heavenly peace, and purity. The divinity's purity is represented by all the followers of this Orïsa wearing white. The divinity has a strong sense of justice, and honor is paramount. This Orïsa's reputation, like their clothes, is spotless. They are known as the king of the white cloth, and, thus, represent divine cleanliness. Obatalá is offered snails, rice, and shea butter by initiates in the religion.

Eshú

Eshú is seen as a trickster guardian of the crossroads. The crossroads here represent both a physical junction between two roads, and a divine midpoint between heaven and earth. The master of liminal, or in-between, spaces, he lives neither in this world nor the next, neither in the human nor the divine realm; a constant intermediary, he is at home everywhere and nowhere. There is a traditional tale concerning Eshú in which he exhibits a ravenous appetite, eats everything his mother brings him, and then eats his mother, too. In response, his horrified father consults Orunmilá and makes the appropriate sacrifices. When Eshú threatens to eat him too, Orunmilá hacks him to pieces that become *yangi*, or pieces of laterite (a red porous clay). Orunmilá then chases him through nine different heavens until, at last, Eshú is appeased and, in addition to returning his mother, he allows each one of the clay shards to become his representatives in the physical world. This story explains Eshú's ability to simultaneously be in many places at once and also demonstrates his power to destroy, or to multiply, depending on whether he is properly worshipped. Proper devotional worship involves leaving the correct offerings at the correct time. Eshú's offerings and accessories are often placed or worn upside-down to salute his backwardness. Each specific manifestation of this Orïsa has its own likes and dislikes, and the devotee has a lifetime of sacred knowledge to internalize.

Wooden statues for Eshú-Odara, the avatar or manifestation known as "the wonder worker," appear in both male and female form and exhibit bulging eyes (which indicate the ability to make things happen) and a blade-like element atop the head (which signals the beginning of his powers). The blade is also used to signify that Eshú is always ready for a kill. As an extraordinary communicator, he assumes the position of cosmic go-between. Through him, humans and otherworldly beings are assured of a means of intercourse or exchange. However, the path he creates is not always direct: one of his names is Aflakete, which roughly means "I have tricked you." He is capable of obfuscating information and manipulating perspective to his own ends. He embodies crossed purposes, crossed speech, and, most of all, the actual crossroads themselves. In simplest terms, the crossroads is the place where heaven and earth meet, but it is also the place where doors open and close, and where opportunities are taken or lost. Eshú walks on the sharp edge of chaos and is never static. He is a trickster because of (rather than in spite of) his commitment to truth and justice. He is not just an elusive character. He is elusion itself, because his job is to actualize potential by making people see things in a new and better light. In yet another Yoruba legend, Eshú is asked why he doesn't speak straightforwardly. Eshú answers, "I never do. I like to make people think."

On his sacred shrine, Eshú is frequently depicted with a red parrot feather on the top of his head as a symbol of great ashé. Eshú-Yangi is the name for "the father of all Eshú," and the oldest artistic representations for him are cones made of laterite that date back to 17th-century Africa. The cones of laterite still appear in Yoruba markets today and serve as a shrine to Eshú. Some believe that laterite cones were transplanted to the Santería, or La Regla Lucumí, tradition in the manner of the concrete heads with cowrie-shell eyes crafted for Elegguá. Eshú is often fed spicy peppers such as jalapeño and black peppercorn. Customarily, a portion of every offering is presented to this divinity first so he can ensure its safe passage to the other Orïsa.

Sango

The brilliance, heat, power, and surprise of fire all embody the Orïsa Sango. Devotees of Sango are said to be children of fire. The man who later became the god is said to have lived as the third or fourth *Alaafin* (king) of the Yoruba people in Oyo (West Africa) well over 1,000 years ago. However, the worship of a lord of fire was probably in existence way before this time. Sango, also known as Esango, is the Orïsa of thunder. He rules by thunder, and his thunderbolts are referred to as thunder axes, which are believed to strike down all those who are unjust. For Sango, both violence and calm assemble in his image. He adores, lives life to the fullest, and takes advantage of every moment. He is highly sexual, logical, and inspiring. As an embodiment of fertility and vigor, he is appealed to by many for success in this area. He is a powerful masculine force of sexuality. A common ritual tool of his is the *ashé sango*, a double-headed axe. This axe is representative of justice and injustice, punishment and death. Some devotional images even feature Sango with this axe as his crown.

Like most Orïsa, his energy has a positive and a negative side. He is often said to provoke jealousy through the power of his penis. The danger is that he does not always choose the best outlets for his attention and creativity, which often turn to gratuitous sex and liquor. Sango is customarily given offerings of greens, bananas, rice, yams, cigars, beans, okra, red and white wine, and bitter kola nut. Ceremonies for him often involve several lively trance-possessions and much dancing and drumming. His shrine can be as impressive as this king himself. The majesty often includes thunderstones, gourds, kola nuts, cowries, and several food offerings. Sango's image is that of the ram, which always takes a place of honor in his shrine.

Osun-Osogbo Sacred Grove in Nigeria. A sacred forest along the banks of the Osun river just outside the city of Osogbo in Osun State. Cultural landscape of undisturbed forest. [Adobe Stock]

Osün

The energy of the river is named Osün. Sweet and sensual, this is the Orïsa of the Osun River in Nigeria. Like her husband Sango, she is frequently honored with lively parties filled with music and dance. For the Yoruba, Osün represents a force with great money and extreme generosity. She is seen as detesting liars and is somewhat prone to jealousy. Among Yoruban Ifá worshippers, her sacred metal is brass. Her ritual jewelry and power items are crafted of brass. It is even believed that she lived in a great brass palace with her first husband, Orunmilá, or Ifá. Her ceremonial animal is frequently the alligator or crocodile, and she is asked to assist with matters of love.

Oshosi

Oshosi, Osossi, or Ochosi is the spirit of the hunter, the tracker, and divine destiny. He is intimately connected to nature and the plants and animals of the forest. He is seen as a skilled herbalist and knows plants with which to heal and harm. With his divine bow and arrow, he guides seekers onto the path of their destiny. As the ultimate tracker, Oshosi is also the divine explorer delving into the sacred mysteries of both the forest and the self. What he finds there is kindness and enlightenment. Oshosi devotees sometimes access the power of the leopard by wearing a leopard skin. This helps them to hunt in both the physical and spiritual worlds. Oshosi is traditionally given offerings of corn, palm oil, and game animals.

Ogou

The god of warfare and the ashé of iron is Ogou, or Ogun. He is the owner of the gun, the knife, the razor, the police and the law, metal, driving, and more. Even swords are called *gu,* or *gubasa,* after Ogou. Inherently fierce and terrible, he therefore occupies a marginal place in society. Deep in the woods, his forge is his true sanctuary. Ogou, a warrior with the divine sword, owns the blood of all sacrifice. Originally, he was associated with the snake and its dangerous power. His worship has increased steadily over time as his patrons have grown to include construction workers, computer programmers, surgeons, taxi drivers, and others. He embodies the power to kill and to heal, and his worshippers sincerely pray, "Ogou, do not fight us." Ogou is the bringer of civilization through his power over technology and the forge. Evidence from missionaries show the worship of Ogou has been taking place for over 250 years, possibly long before, as early records are not complete or comprehensive.

Ogou devotees in Africa traditionally wear miniature iron implements or hang these items from their sacred staves to honor the Orïsa. These include small anvils, hammers, knives, spears, swords, bells, and pokers. The shrines for Ogou among the Yoruba feature the colors white or red. Offerings of sacrificial meat of chicken, snail, elephant's tail, and rum are sometimes left. His ritual area is often the forest or the railroad track, and it is at these sites where his ritual offerings should be placed.

Oyá and the Egungun

The ashé of the wind and the goddess of change is called Oyá. Seen as the powerful mistress of the dead, she walks with pride and confidence. In Nigeria, she is saluted as the Orïsa of the Niger River. She carries with her the abundance of monumental change. She is also traditionally revered as the owner of the marketplace. In Africa, many of these market sites are traditionally dominated by women, where they sell their wares and create a universe crafted to their own liking. In representations, Oyá dances her whirlwind of suddenness with such force that she is known to discharge electric sparks. The spirit of the wind, she is frequently given offerings of eggplant, red grapes, and red wine. Her number is 9, so items are usually left in combinations of the number. Oyá is one of the few Orïsa allowed to wear dark colors; as such, her ritual colors are purple and sometimes even black. Among the Yoruba, she is frequently associated with the Egungun societies for the ancestors. These societies appear masked during ritual and, for this reason, altars to Oyá can sometimes feature ceremonial masks.

The Egungun are the spirits of the honored dead. They are believed to travel back from the land of the dead to visit the living and bring messages and advice. Secret societies are formed to pay tribute to these ancestors, and a monthlong festival is held in their honor. During the festival, participants are heavily costumed in beaded finery, or *raffia* (straw), and masked, and they dance with horsetail whips in large swirling motions. Eventually, they slip into trance-possessions and give blessings and judgments to those who are present.

Yemonja, Olokun, Nana Buruku

Yemonja, or Yemoja, is the mistress of the sea. The mother of several of the other Orïsa, she is the sister of Oshun.

She is described as both nurturing and devouring, dark and radiant. She is seen as part of the Orïsa Olokun in some variations of the religion, while others separate the two deities. The title *Olokun* roughly translates to "owner of the ocean." Yemonja and Olokun bring worshippers fertility, prosperity, and wealth. Whereas Yemonja is the mother of the fishes, it is said of Olokun that "no one knows what truly lies at the bottom of the ocean." Both Orïsa exist side by side in the watery realm. On their altars,

Olokun and Yemonja are usually represented with images relating to the ocean. The sacred art for Yemonja includes *abebe*, or rounded fans, which are used to capture her ashé of cool water. Shaped like a giant drop of water, they are said to restore calm to any situation. Both Orïsa are fond of silver stars, moons, and bells. They dress in coral, and lizards or chameleons are sacred to them. Olokun shrines are almost always located outdoors, often featuring mirrors to symbolize the ocean and to aid in trance. Ladders are sometimes included because they represent the spiritual ascension that is made possible through Olokun.

Nana Buruku, or Nana Buukun, is a strong and ancient Orïsa who symbolizes the "mother without children." She raises these children even if she hasn't physically birthed them herself. This mother of everything is responsible for both small children and the hearth. Revered not just among the Yoruba, this deity represents female courage, grand knowledge, and power. Nana Buruku is said to be the mother of the Ibeji and Obaluaiye, or Babaluaiye (Yoruba). She is a warrior woman who carries an *ileeshin*, or magickal staff. She is often covered in raffia, similar to the clothing of her son, Sonponno (West Africa) or Babaluaiye.

Sonponno and Mami Wata

The divinity made famous in the United States by Desi Arnaz is the Yoruba Babaluaiye. Among the Fon people of West Africa, this god of sickness is known as Sonponno, or Sakpata. Originally respected because of his ability to cure— or magickally conjure up—smallpox, his priests were accused by the British government of spreading the disease during the late-19th century. He involves the terror of sudden illness and has recently become associated with HIV/AIDS and COVID-19. Occasionally, a person possessed by Sonponno will give a lecture on condom use and other medical safeties. Shrines for Sonponno are usually housed outside the home, and even outside the village. His shrine often contains several small gourds in which he is said to place his medicines.

Mami Wata is a joyous goddess who represents the sea. She is often depicted as a mermaid or with an image of the Hindu deity Krishna. When she comes to an initiate during possession, she covers her face with white powder and dances ecstatically. Her shrine must be kept absolutely clean at all times. Rather than being relegated to a specific body of water, she represents all forms of water everywhere.

SACRED ART
YORUBA AND OTHER AFRICAN ROOTS

Art has always been one of the clearest expressions of Yoruba sacred culture. Since the 15th century and even possibly before, Orïsa devotees have been creating beautiful sacred items as an important part of their religion. Frequently, these items are sculptural in form and, over time, become increasingly imbued with the ashé of the Orïsa.

These revered items often attracted the attention of Europeans. In the early 19th century, a ritual Sango staff for the lord of fire and thunder had traveled all the way to Switzerland. The commodification of items like these, unfortunately, has continued throughout history, and large collections of Yoruba ritual art can be found in the hands of collectors, rather than practitioners, in Great Britain, Germany, and the United States.

Many Western scholars have taken up the study of this art and found their way to the study of the religion. Robert Farris Thompson from Yale University writes extensively on this topic. In his book *Flash of the Spirit*, he examines African and African Diasporic art and philosophy by connecting the artistic elements.

YORUBA SACRED MUSIC AND DANCE

Sacred dance is a beautiful and divine manifestation of Yoruba Orïsa worship, also known as Ifá. Practitioners frequently dance to honor the Orïsa. The movements for Eshú, the trickster god, favor the left side of the body, while for Ogou, the lord of iron, the shoulder blades are rhythmically raised and lowered as the head remains motionless. The dances are frequently dictated by the drum rhythms played to call the Orïsa. The dance steps are repetitive and designed to induce trance-possession events that bless and heal the community.

The Afonga, or Fonga, is probably the most popular Yoruba-based rhythm and dance in the world. Beginners learn to chant its simple-yet-powerful words:

Afonga Alafia Ashé Ashé
Afonga Alafia Ashé Ashé
Ashé Ashé
Ashé Ashé
Afonga Alafia Ashé Ashé

Afonga is the name of the dance chant, while *Alafia* translates roughly to mean "peace and blessings." As previously stated, *Ashé* is spiritual power, sacred energy, and divine grace. This is a wonderful chant to use in prayer to gain focus and clarity. The Yoruba word for sacrifice is ebo. Linguistically, it breaks down into the words "to feed" and "to worship." Sacrifice, both animal and otherwise, is employed by initiated members of the community to please the Orïsa. Just like humans, the Orïsa need to eat and pray. Prayer is viewed as the highest form of sacrifice and is employed by Ifá worshippers on a regular basis.

YORUBA CALENDAR

A Yoruba religious calendar, especially one based on traditional beliefs, is impossible to devise. The original calendar, which was in place hundreds of years ago, had a four-day week. Orïsa were rotated and honored according to a schedule. For example, the middle of the week was always market time and used to honor the Orïsa Oyá, the mistress of the marketplace. Today, this historically oral tradition has a calendar with days like Tuesday as Ojo Isogons (day of victory), or Wednesday as Ojo riru Ojooru (day of confusion). These are modern adaptations to coincide with the Western way of configuring things. Suffice to say, there is no Yoruba religious calendar corresponding to the Gregorian (Western/Christian) calendar.

YORUBAN SACRED STORIES

Everything about the trickster Orïsa Eshú is confusing and contrary. One common saying tells us that "Eshú lies down in bed and bumps his head on the ceiling." The most popular myth about Eshú concerns a two-colored hat.

> *Eshú was walking down the road one day when he overheard two brothers on opposite sides of the road talking. The brothers were dressed alike, had the same mannerisms, and appeared to be close friends.*
>
> *The first brother said, "Thank you, my brother, for helping me with my crops and for living so close by so I can borrow your tools. You are a very good brother."*
>
> *The second brother replied, "You are welcome, my brother. Thank you for your help with my farm and for letting me store my grain with yours. The crops look wonderful. You are a very good brother."*
>
> *All this harmony made Eshú quite nauseous, so he decided to stick his crooked cane into the situation. He got a hat that was colored black on one side and white on the other. He put it on and proceeded to walk straight down the road between the two brothers. One brother said to the other, "Did you see that guy with the black hat?" The other brother replied, "I only saw a man with a white hat. What are you talking about?" An argument quickly ensued. Soon, the brothers were fighting and destroying their farms. This affected the food supply for the whole kingdom, and it wasn't long before the king got involved. He ordered the people to find Eshú and bring him back so he could be punished for causing so much trouble. As always, Eshú was a few steps ahead of them. He had decided to leave the kingdom. As he left, however, he set fire to the houses he passed. When people ran out of their homes carrying their belongings, he offered to keep an eye on them. He then gave the stuff to the next passerby, scattering the people's possessions all across the land.*

According to the mythology of the Yoruba, in the beginning of time, the world was born in water and marshland. The Orïsa lived in the sky and would travel down to earth on glistening spiderwebs to play and enjoy themselves. Olodumare, the creator deity, decided one day to create some firm earth amid the marsh. He sent the Orïsa Nla, perhaps a permutation of the Orïsa Orunla, to the world below with a snail shell containing a pigeon and a hen. Nla placed the birds down on the marshland, and they kicked up a storm. Scratching and digging, they continued until the land began to form. Olodumare then sent a sacred chameleon down to the ground to inspect the work. It is said the chameleon reported the ground to be "still too watery." Nla was sent to work again to make sure the land was both wide and dry.

When he stopped, the city of Ile Ife had been created. The name translates roughly to "wide home." Ile Ife has been the actual center of Yoruba sacred culture for hundreds of years.

YORUBA BOTANICALS

The following is a partial list of items that can be left as *adimu* (nonanimal offerings) for the Orïsa. They can be obtained from any good herbal store or online. Whenever possible, the Yoruba names have been given in addition to the English ones.

Anis—Blessings, peace

Coconut *(Agbon)*—Peace

Bitter kola *(Orogbo)*—Luck

Millet *(Baba)*—Fertility

Onion *(Alubosa)*—Protection against evil

Olive oil—Good all-purpose oil for offerings

Palm oil—Offered to many of the Orïsa, to give direction

Pumpkin seeds—Fertility, success

Shea butter *(Ori)*—Calm, wisdom

UNCERTAIN FUTURE

For decades, there has been great political and economic unrest in Nigeria. Like the previous Eshú story, people and things have been scattered across the land. Up until the mid-1990s, several practitioners from North and South America returned to Nigeria to receive spiritual instruction. Today, that is not so easy. Several of the priests and priestesses of the religion have settled in Europe, particularly the Netherlands, and in the Americas. This spreading of the traditions has unfortunately made things more difficult in many ways, so please do your best to verify the authenticity of any practitioner you are consulting for divination or initiations.

CHAPTER TWO
HAITIAN VODOU
EFFECTIVE POWER

Despite years of economic strife, political oppression, and outside intervention, the religion of Vodou (this is the Haitian form of religion, not to be confused with Voodoo of New Orleans) continues to thrive in the country of Haiti. The inhabitants of the island, originally called Santo Domingo, still follow their foremothers' and forefathers' religion: Vodou. The etymology of the word *Vodou* is known to come from words meaning "spirit," "deity," or "effective power."

As part of Vodou, followers honor the Lwa, or Loa (divinities). The Lwa are thought of as parents, spouses, mentors, angels, devils, Les Mystères (mysteries), and Les Invisibles (invisibles). Depended on in times of trouble and saluted in times of joy, the Lwa are there for worshippers, provided they know the proper drawings, songs, and rhythms to call them.

The hounfor is the ritual center for all Vodou practices. It includes not only buildings to hold shrines but also sacred trees, gardens, and areas for healing and livestock. There are hundreds of hounfor throughout Haiti and the world beyond, and each one is slightly different. In the city, space is likely to be at a premium and, often, sacred areas are forced to exist on a smaller scale or in a more mobile form. The ritual areas can be spartan or heavily ornate. It all depends on the temple's aesthetic taste and the ancestral guidelines that have been laid out for them. Each hounfor does have a center pole, called the *poteau mitan*. Sometimes, this is the actual support beam for the entire structure. The pole, which is believed to rotate on its axis between heaven and earth, functions as a spiritual lightning rod that allows the Lwa to focus in on the hounfor. Occasionally, it can be a chain, rather than a piece of wood or a living tree. In any case, it is used as the center of the ritual area, and *vévés* (ritual ground drawings) and offerings are placed around the base. I know of one priest who had a poteau mitan made of harvested wood that was alive with termites. He saw this as a blessing from the Gede, or unnamed ancestors, who often manifest in insect form. At the time, I did not share his amazement, but it was still interesting to hear them alive and traveling inside the pole.

A mambo and houngan are responsible for running the hounfor and the rituals that occur there. Still, their actual role is so pervasive that it defies explanation. They are mother and father, pope and papess for the temple members who turn to them for assistance in all areas of life.

VODOU HISTORY
FROM ENSLAVED PEOPLE TO GODS

The island originally named Haiti by its indigenous Taino and Arawak residents was renamed Hispaniola when it was aggressively taken by Christopher Columbus for Spain in 1492. The native people of the island were cruelly destroyed by maltreatment, illness, and forced labor in the mines. Their impressive number of approximately 1.3 million had dwindled to only 60,000 just 15 years later. Slaves from Africa were imported to the island beginning in 1503 to carry out the crushing work of the native residents. This population eventually grew to almost half a million. What culminated was a successful slave revolution in 1804 empowered by Vodou.

The Vodou initiation system here is complex and involves many different levels. The beginning ceremony performed on devotees is the Lavé Tet, or headwashing. Then, depending on the hounfor, the devotee goes through various stages, such as *hounsi bosalle, hounsi canzo (kanzo)*, and finally leading up to becoming a mambo or houngan, followed by further initiations if necessary.

THE LWA

The total number of Lwa are too numerous to describe here. In addition, their ranks are ever-changing, because any of the honored dead can eventually, with time and attention, become Lwa.

In Haiti, the religion is organized according to *nanchons,* or family lineages. The nanchons are groups of Lwa that are seen as belonging to the same original tribal lineage. The nanchons are categorized according to different tribal groups whose members were captured and forcibly brought to the Americas. The slaves from the same village or region were typically not kept in the same holding area. As such, problems with language and customs between the captured developed. In the newly formed groups composed of people from many tribes, the individual members concentrated on those parts of their religions that were similar. Some of the most prominent of the nanchons are Petro, Congo, Ibo, and Rada. The Petro family of spirits are said to be hot, quick, and fiery. Moving with sharp motions, they are considered by some to be a unique line indigenous to the Haitian Creole-speaking people themselves. The Petro are counterbalanced by the Congo spirits, which are much more watery, joyful, and cool and are theorized by some to be of Bantu origin. The Ibo spirits descended from the Hausa, Benin, and Yoruba empires. The Rada spirits are believed to have originated in Dahomey in West Africa and are said to have a more airy and gentle nature. There are, however, no absolutes. As a whole, Vodou has been moving toward less of a nanchon-defined structure of ritual and more of a Lwa-inspired one. Individuals still pay tribute to their family Lwa, but in group ceremonies many different Lwa from varying nanchons are honored. The following are the most-often-worshipped entities.

Legba

Papa Legba is probably the most prevalent and frequently petitioned deity. A common salute says "Open the road, open the gate, open the door. We wish to come home Papa." Legba is the wise father, the king of all kings, seen as the paternal force of creation in the universe. He is most often envisioned as an old man with a cane. The cane, representative of his penis, has become so old that it has now become his walking stick that he uses to plant his seed in the earth. A divine intermediary, he stands firmly at the crossroads transporting messages from the visible world to the invisible and vice versa. All practitioners must go past Legba to have contact with the other Lwa, and he is called at the start of almost every ceremony. Some practitioners equate his energy with that of the brilliant sunshine. As a tribute, Papa Legba is frequently offered rum, coffee, peanuts, cigars, spicy corn fritters, smoked foods, and hard candy. He is almost always represented in the hounfor with a cane, but some also use the Catholic image of Saint Peter due to his connection with the holy keys to the gates of heaven, or with the image of Moses. To salute him, a devotee often kisses, or knocks on, the ground three times and asks him to open the door to the world of the invisible. Legba trance-possession events traditionally involve one walking slightly hunched or with a cane.

His traditional colors are red and black, or white and black, symbolizing the connection and confusion associated with straddling the earth and the sky.

Erzulie

There are many Erzulies. The Erzulie of the Rada rites is called Erzulie Freda, a Lwa whose domain is water and whose dwelling place is waterfalls and riverbanks. Her symbolic colors are light blue and pink, although her clothing may also be rose-colored or white. Tuesday and Thursday are her special days. Among the flora and fauna sacred to Erzulie Freda are the laurel tree, all sweet-smelling flowers (particularly roses and jasmine), the white dove, and the herb basil. In fact, she demands cleanliness of her children at all times. Alternatively, in another manifestation as Maîtresse (Mistress) Erzulie, she is envisioned as a coquette of exceptional beauty, grace, and sensuality and as a lady of great luxury. Three wedding bands adorn her fingers simultaneously for Damballa (the serpent god), Agwé (the lord of the fisherman), and Ogou (the god of iron). This situation is not looked on as promiscuity but rather as proof of her largeness of heart. Her favorite offerings include refined or gourmet dishes with delicately seasoned sauces, small cakes or other sweet confections, expensive perfumes, fresh flowers, toiletries and cosmetics, jewelry of gold and/or of pearls, honey, bananas, sweet liqueurs such as crème de menthe, and (her special favorite) champagne, which is always kept in readiness for her appearance. Her primary symbols are a heart, a mirror, and a fan, but tears or uncontrollable weeping are also an essential part of her character. These can be tears of sadness, joy, or frustration, each representing a different facet of Erzulie.

Although the many avatars of Erzulie are too numerous to list here in their entirety, the following are a few of the more commonly recognized faces of this Lwa. Under the following names she has come to represent help, good will, health, beauty, fortune, and love: Erzulie Severine Belle Femme (beautiful woman), La Belle Femme (Venus), La Grande Erzulie (elderly, grieving woman, identified with Saint Anne), and Tsilah Wedo (beauty, peace, and wealth). Still, Erzulie is also a goddess of jealousy, vengeance, and discord as personified by the following aspects: Erzulie Toho, Erzulie Zandor, Erzulie Mapiangueh, and Erzulie Ge-Rouge. One particularly interesting aspect of Erzulie is Erzulie Dantor (Ezili Danto), a country woman, who is conflated with the Catholic Black Madonnas such as the Mater Salvatoris. The child she holds is understood to be a daughter named Anaïs. This Petro Lwa wears red and blue and, reflecting her country origins, her offerings may include raw rum, *griyo* (fried pork), and unfiltered cigarettes. Black pigs are sacred to her, which puts one in mind of the sacrificial black pig used in the legendary Bois-Caiman ceremony of rebellion (August 1791), when Boukman implored his fellow countrymen to listen to the voice of liberty in their hearts in the name of the ancestral gods of Africa.

Damballa and Aida Wedo

Damballa, Damballa Wedo, or Damballa Hwedo is traditionally seen as the serpent creator in the Haitian tradition. A serpent of pure white, he is seen as an ancient force in the religion. When he manifests during possession, he writhes on the ground and does not make any sound except hissing and gagging noises. In some hounfor, the center pole is referred to as the poteau Damballa. Papa Damballa travels beneath the waters, creating and caring for his vast stores of memory. Damballa is owner of the divine waters of heaven and is honored in matters of love, knowledge, healing, and wealth. Often, the Catholic lithograph for Saint Patrick is used to represent this Lwa. This could be attributed to the fact that the image features a wise, authoritative Saint Patrick replete with white hair and beard and coiling serpents at his feet. The image of Moses is also used for its serpent imagery. Damballa's offerings are almost always white: white rice, eggs, flour, and milk are all appropriate, as are pineapple, white grapes, olive oil, and sweet wine. He is honored by devotees on Wednesday or Thursday. There is an avatar of Damballa for the Petro nanchon of Lwa called Damballa La Flambeau. This snake strikes with a tongue and a tail of divine fire. This particular avatar is overtly sexual. The first drum ceremony I held for this Lwa sparked a chant among the crowd of "Damballa La Flambeau—the fire down below."

Aida Wedo, or Ayida Ouido, is the wife of Damballa. Most often envisioned as a rainbow sky serpent, she brings her followers love and understanding. She is offered eggs and other white items painted in rainbow colors. Silent and nurturing, she coils around her husband in a double helix of sensual perfection. Together, Damballa and Aida are the great parents of us all, holding the mysteries of life and death. Like the Ouroboros, or sacred serpent circle, they are representative of the perfect organic machine. The snakes take us with them along the curving journey of life, spinning us toward necessary beginnings and endings.

Marassa and Gran Bois

Each different manifestation of Traditional African Religion has its own version of divine twins. They are seen as the sacred male and female forces in the universe. In Haitian Vodou, they are referred to as the Marassa. One way to describe them to those unfamiliar with the tradition is to imagine them as a Vodou variation of the Chinese principles of yin and yang. They are not, strictly speaking, Lwa, but rather forces in the universe that precede creation and make it possible for things to be born into being. In Haiti, they are described as Mawu, a female child, and Lisa, a male child. They are responsible for joy, happiness, and divine balance. The Marassa are given offerings of candy and toys on their shrines and during ceremonies. There are several different manifestations of the Marassa within the Haitian pantheon: the Marassa, the Marassa dosu, the Marassa trois, and even a set of Marassa quadruplets. They are fed offerings in special double- or triple-sided bowls made of monkey pod wood.

The Lwa of the forest is called Gran Bois, or Ganja Bois. His fingers and toes are roots that reach deep into the earth to gain wisdom and nourishment. The land he resides in is the abode of the recently dead. He controls the sacred herbal medicines and preparations of the woods. Because his domain is the forest, the large Haitian population in Brooklyn, N.Y., has chosen to leave many of his offerings in Prospect Park. Gran Bois is most often envisioned as the wise old avuncular figure with roots for fingers and toes. He speaks in rhyme and knows all the powerful secrets of the herbs. Gran Bois is one of the few Lwa responsible for conferring the *asson*, or ritual rattle, to the mambo or houngan.

Ayizan and Papa Loko

Ayizan is seen as the Lwa of initiation. She is given offerings of palm fronds and crab. Her energy is that of love and success. She drinks no alcohol but is instead offered other beverages such as peach nectar. The imagery that is found on her altar relates to hearts. When she appears during possession trance, she conducts herself with divine grace and elegance.

Known as Papa Loko, or Loco Attisou, this Lwa is the ancient priest, the guardian of the hounfor. As the husband to Ayizan, he in many ways signifies the support of the community. Loko simultaneously represents agriculture and nature as the deity of the center pole and the sacred mapou tree. His colors are white and red, which symbolize the primal fluids of man and woman, namely semen and menstrual blood.

Very rarely does Loko possess someone, but when he does, he can be recalcitrant and refuse to assist the congregation with their problems. He is not a Lwa to be angered and is known to break things if ritual rules are not followed. Luckily, if he is pleased, he can diagnose illnesses and prescribe herbal cures. Since he is the ruler of the priesthood and initiations, houngans turn to him during ceremony for inspiration, guidance, and fortitude. He is almost as important as Papa Legba, as Loko's assistance is vital to the success of any ritual. He is most often honored on Wednesday, and the Catholic lithograph most often used for him is Saint Joseph the Worker.

Loko and his wife, Ayizan, are sacred paternal Lwa functioning to assist with healings, initiations, and instruction. Together, they form a divine union of male and female, priest and priestess, uniting to guide and advise the community.

Azaka and Gran Ibo

Azaka, Azaka Mede, or Kouzin is a Lwa that seems to have carried on in the more agricultural communities of Haiti while falling out of favor with the more urbanized societies. Like many of the Lwa, they are often seen alternately as male or female, depending on the situation. Typical field hands, they wear blue jeans and a striped shirt, frequently accented with a patterned red kerchief and a straw hat. Very much the county fieldworkers, they know deeply the value of hard work and the fertile blessings of the land. Some devotees associate them with Saint Isidore, the patron saint of farmers, who is depicted with blue pants and a satchel. Azaka is always humble, a simple and shy, illiterate farmer, and they both remind the congregation of their spiritual and physical roots. Likewise, temples in both rural and urban Haiti regularly include a dirt floor, again reinforcing a deep connection to the earth. This Lwa's traditional colors are blue and white. Azaka is the brother of the Gede and frequently shows up at Gede rituals, where he is offered raw sugarcane, rice and beans, cola, rum, gin, tequila, scotch, popcorn, candy, peanuts, and various grains. They straddle the two worlds of family and business, making a connection between the two. When they enter a possessed person, their voice sounds like a goat. Their day is Saturday.

The goddess Gran Ibo is seen as the great mistress, the grandmother, the old wise woman of the swamp. She speaks rarely; when she does, it is often in tongues, telling anyone who will listen everything and nothing, and she is ultimately the way to salvation. This is one of the Ibo spirits, belonging to people descended from the Hausa, Benin, and Yoruba empires, many of whom are still revered today among the Gullah people of South Carolina's seacoast.

Bossou, ShiLiBo, and Blanc Dani

The Lwa of the bull is called Bossou. Envisioned as strong and warlike, he comes to the aid of the congregation when fortitude is required. When a member of the Vodou congregation is possessed by Bossou, he or she frequently tries to mount everyone in attendance. This mounting behavior is a primal and animalistic attempt to establish dominance. He is believed to have a certain power over life and death, which he may reveal in a ritual mirror, if he so desires. His colors are red, white, and black, and he eats beef. The Catholic image used for him is Saint Vincent de Paul.

ShiLiBo, or Silibo, is the Lwa of pure joy. She is like the first manifestation of bliss and the unification and power of great knowledge. As a representative of elation, she stands naked and glistening in the sunshine with copper-colored skin and long tresses. She is the vestal virgin and, as such, is traditionally represented by images of the Virgin Mary. ShiLiBo is offered sunflower seeds and water from a bubbling fresh spring. Her ritual number is 6, and her day is Tuesday.

In Vodou, there are frequently several different sacred serpents. Blanc Dani is another one of them. This is a Lwa of peace and serene calm. Like Damballa, Blanc Dani is envisioned as a white snake.

LaSirene

The beautiful, watery mistress of the sea is called LaSirene, or Lasiren. Her sweet songs lead followers to both marriage and dangerous distraction. Images frequently depict her as a mermaid granting gifts of great wealth. According to some believers, she is an aspect of Erzulie, while others associate her with a Lwa called La Baleen, the Lwa of whales. Her ritual colors are blue and green. LaSirene is offered pieces of blue sea glass, combs, sacred chants and songs, pink champagne, and sweet white wine. Some say she is the wife of Agwé and the mistress of Ogou, thus being able to please many men with her seductive power. Those fortunate enough to see LaSirene are said to be extremely lucky.

Masa and Simbi

The spirit energy referred to as Masa La Flambeau embodies a playful rebalancing of magickal fire. Fire is viewed as a powerful magickal element in Vodou and is used to transform and cleanse. Masa's purging purification attracts some and paralyzes others.

Simbi is another sacred serpent deity in the tradition of Vodou. Simbi's domain is the watery realms of magick and mystery. Simbi's colors are white and green. The véve for Simbi shows a snake slithering across the crossroads. Some people believe Simbi to be simply another manifestation of Damballa. Simbi's energy, however, seems more electric than Damballa's and is said to represent technology. One of Simbi's manifestations is called Simbi Andezo and is honored with the following Creole song:

Simbi Andezo,

Sa ki fe yo pa vie we mwen …
Simbi Andezo
The reason they don't see me
is because they do not know me … yet
They gave me a spell so that I can walk at night.

The name Simbi Andezo comes from the Creole word for "two waters." This Simbi is shy and slithers between two different watery realms: the one of the living and the one of the dead.

Barons and Gede: The Ancestors

Ancestor worship is a large part of the Haitian tradition, and most often these energies are revered in the form of a group called Les Gede and Les Barons. Lusty and lewd, this legion was described by anthropologist and filmmaker Maya Deren as both "corpse and phallus." These energies of the dead manifest in ritual and behave obscenely, steal or beg for money, dress in shabby or flashy clothes, speak in a nasal twang, and are capable of anything. Everyone has a bit of the energy of the Gede imbedded in their souls as ancestral knowledge. Their energy is almost pervasive or infectious. Sequined and sunglassed, top-hatted and trifling, these entities are known to invade other ceremonies and refuse to leave without some sort of compensation, either financial or flirtatiously sexual. Their appearance is not soon forgotten, as they are known to grab genitalia, bump, grind, curse, and spit—all the while, they are trying to pick your pocket or maybe even your nose. Some hounfor describe the league of departed spirits Les Barons as the named dead, and Les Gede as the unnamed dead. Others make no real distinction between the two groups and see them both as the revered dead and worthy of tribute. They are numerous, the most well-known being Baron Samedi, Maman Brigitte, Baron Criminal, Ti Malice, and Gede Nibo.

Baron Samedi, often referred to as the first male buried in every cemetery, is the ruler of all the dead. He is frequently seen dressed in a top hat and sunglasses, with one eye poking out of them. This is said to represent the fact that he has one eye at watch in both worlds, and also alludes to the sexual implications of a "one-eyed wonder," or penis. This Baron is in many ways the stereotypical face of Vodou. He is offered rum, cigars, hot peppers, spare change, and flashy jewelry. Baron Samedi is honored on Saturday.

Maman Brigitte is the wife of the Baron. She is also known as Mademoiselle Brigitte and Gran Brigitte. Analogously, she is known as "the first woman interred in a cemetery." She possesses her own special power over a mother's justice and joy. She resides in the cemetery's trees and rock piles and is seen as highly sensual. Often shrouded in the wisdom that is born in silence, she sometimes inspires her devotees to stuff their noses and mouths with cotton. Spirit possessions by her in her foremother form are rare. However, I was told once by a member of a different tradition that they were contacted by a manifestation of Ti Brigitte, a young girl with a short skirt who liked to show off her panties. Ultimately, she is a divine arbiter of justice, and practitioners petition her concerning legal cases. A loose connection can be seen between her and the Celtic goddess Brigit. Honored with the light of several candles, she is offered cotton, rum, oranges, and willow branches.

Baron Criminal is seen as a force of justice for criminals. Sometimes seen as just a face of Baron Samedi, other hounfor revere him as a sort of spiritual police waiting in the wings to eat people as soon as they make a wrong turn. He is often symbolized by a cross.

One of the popular Gede spirits is called Ti Malice (Uncle Malice), who is said to be both unlucky and mischievous. Ti Malice has a giant ass that farts often and can talk. Shrines for the Gede may feature antique scales believed to assist them in the weighing of souls. They are frequently offered nutmeg, black pepper, alcohol, peanuts, corn, and cassava.

Gede Nibo is an entity who is seen as a gravedigger. He is lustily sexual and is said to have a cinnamon anus, which is indicative of his flamboyant sexuality. He is also referred to as Ti Puce (Uncle Louse).

Agwé

Agwé is a patron of fisherpeople and the sea. The vévé for him is that of a ship. The ship is so strong and powerful that it can weather any storm. When practitioners use the image of a saint to represent him, it is that of Saint Ulrich. Other images show him as a light-skinned person with hazel eyes. Agwé always wears a naval dress uniform with a helmet and gloves.

He is offered champagne and other expensive drinks. Seen as a perfect spouse, Agwé is always supportive. He is married to the Lwa LaSirene, yet some believe he has other wives as well. Altars frequently contain offerings of small boats, anchors, steamboats, warships, boat oars, fish, nets, and other symbols of the sea.

Ogou

Believed to have been the patron deity for Jean-Jacques Dessalines (a leader of the Haitian Revolution), the deity Ogou, or Ogun, is therefore afforded a privileged place within the Haitian religion. A frequent reminder in the African religious traditions, this Lwa will not tolerate injustice. There are several different manifestations of Ogou that occur within Vodou. As Ogou Feray or Ogun Feraille, a fierce warrior and no stranger to battle, he serves to protect the community. Unlike some of the other African Diasporic Religions, the color here for Ogou is not green, but red. Representative of the spirit of iron, he is a revolutionary and a soldier integral to Haitian independence. Ogou Bahlindo is the Ogou for healing. In a country frequently plagued by hunger, earthquakes, and—more recently—disease, this deity has become increasingly popular. Ogou La Flambeau is the war-damaged madman. He is the soldier with the flaming machete who dines on bullets and hot blood. Fighting everything and everyone, this is a fierce Lwa that is summoned only in times of deep despair. Sometimes this Lwa is represented with the Catholic lithograph for Saint Jacques. Ogou's shrine is often covered in red velvet and contains a machete or other ritual knife or sword, a rake, spade, and yams.

SPIRIT MARRIAGE
TO LIE WITH THE LWA

The Vodou religion has a special provision for initiates who need to enhance their connection with the Lwa: spirit marriage. An individual does not choose to undergo this ceremony but is instead chosen directly by the Lwa themselves. The practitioner is called on through trance-possession, dreams, and occasionally illness or even financial tragedy. I have even heard of cases where they demand devotees to perform this type of marriage before they are allowed to complete one in the secular world. It is only after these trials, either directly or via consultation with a mambo or houngan, that the need for a spiritual wedding is revealed.

The actual ceremony is often preceded by another ceremony: the Lavé Tet. After that is done, the whole ceremony actually resembles a traditional Christian wedding. An individual acts as priest, sometimes even speaking in Latin, wedding rings are conferred, and a marriage license is even filled out. The licenses are easily obtained throughout Haiti for a nominal fee. However, the entire ritual itself can be quite expensive, as the betrothed must pay for rings, appropriate clothing, musicians, a cake, and the accompanying grand wedding feast.

A special room in the hounfor is set aside for wedding preparations and the eventual consecration of the union. In the days leading up to the ritual, the spouse-to-be is instructed in the complex knowledge necessary for the sacred marriage. This information consists of the specific Lwa's favorite foods, herbs, songs, colors, rhythms, and chants, which all must be memorized by the devotee.

The ceremony consists of hours of dancing, drumming, and feasting for the Lwa. During this time, the betrothed spends his or her time lying motionless in seclusion waiting for the Lwa to arrive. If the Lwa feels pleased by the offerings, he or she agrees to the union by possessing either the spouse or another member of the hounfor. Then the wedding proper will begin. The priest will say the vows, and the mambo and houngan will sign as witnesses to the union.

Once the ceremony is complete, the spouse will abstain from sexual relations on his or her Lwa's day of the week, reserving that time for his or her divine mate. If he or she has the space in his or her home, an entire room may be dedicated to that Lwa. This is representative of the level of commitment that Vodou followers are willing to go to for their religion.

The spirit marriage is arguably one of the most important practices in Vodou. Even the Haitian Creole word for the ritual assistant of Vodou, *hounsi*, literally means "wife." The hounsi make up the bulk of the congregation, functioning as ritual dancers and a ceremonial chorus. The Lwa that most often enter into this sprit marriage arrangement are Erzulie,

Damballa, Agwé, Gede, and Ogou. Through these unions, both hounsi and Lwa alike are able to strengthen their bond with another world.

POLITICAL HISTORY

The political history of Haiti has been tumultuous for hundreds of years. In 1835, the penal code made Vodou rites and practices illegal and remained in effect for over 150 years. Despite the country's amazing revolt against slavery, its people's freedom has always been curtailed. U.S. occupation of Haiti began in 1915 and lasted until 1934. Papa Doc Duvalier came to power in 1957, and a 30-year reign of terror began. The dictator dressed in black and did everything he could in order to liken himself to Baron Samedi, the spirit of the dead. Papa Doc and his son, Baby Doc, were responsible for hundreds, possibly thousands, of deaths. The horror was so extreme that when the Duvalier reign ended, people blamed the Vodou community for the years of horror, and approximately 100 Vodou houngans and mambos were tortured and killed. Sacred hounfor were burned to the ground. Most, if not all, of these people had little or no connection with the Duvaliers. At least 13 priests were forced to recant their Vodou beliefs and declare their faith in Christianity. Those who refused to recant were hacked to death with a machete. U.S. intervention in Haiti occurred again in the 1990s. Vodou finally became a recognized religion in the country in 2003.

VODOU ART

There is a long artistic tradition associated with the Vodou religion. It includes *vévés*, metalwork, and painting. A lot of the creations stem from the fact that while the Haitian people may not have vast financial resources, they have vast creative talent. People make art with whatever they can to honor the Lwa, and what results are some of the most stunning creations in the world.

Vévés are often created on the open ground in cornmeal, flour, rice powder, Red Brick Dust, coffee, gunpowder, or other materials. Each Lwa has his or her own unique vévé that is, in part, open to aesthetic interpretation on the part of the creator. The design serves as a spiritual conduit for all who come into contact with it. Forming a sacred gateway, it ensures the safe journey of all who dance on the astral path. This astral path travels between the physical world of humanity and the divine world of the Lwa.

The word "vévé" is derived from the ancient Fon (also known as the Dahomey of West Africa) people's term for "ritual palm oil" used in rectangular-shaped ground offerings for the deities. Similar drawings can be found among the Congo people, the Ndembu tribal people of Zambia, and the Pende tribal people of Zaire. The ritual *vévés* of Vodou, however, are more detailed than those found in Africa. V*évés* often honor multiple Lwa and incorporate symbols from many different traditions and practices.

Legba flag vévé. – [photo by author]

The eloquent artistry of the *vévé* is primal and divine. In some spiritual houses, the lines are drawn simultaneously with both hands, representative of their reaching equally into both worlds. Their thickness and thinness varies with each particular drawing. They can be created to honor a single Lwa, or many *vévés* can be combined. As the ceremony begins, the dancers begin to move about in their bare feet over the *vévés*, absorbing the *vévés*' ashé into their feet, which passes through their body and then their souls to bless and guide the participants. Sometimes, after the ceremony, the *vévés* are cleaned up with the rest of the offerings and deposited on the bare earth, typically under a large tree.

Wall vévé on display at Haiti Cultural Exchange. – [photo by author]

Vévés, as stated, were originally utilized solely as ground drawings but have become multifunctional over time. Metal *vévés* serving as permanent offerings to the spirits became popular in the early years of the 20th century and are still sold today. These range from simple to intensely complex hand-hammered metal cutouts. They are created to bring the Lwa into a house or temple when they are hung on the wall. Some of the more notable artists in this venue are Georges Littaud and Gabriel Ben-Aime.

Sequin flags are a ritual form that is unique to Haitian Vodou. These elaborate creations are a feature of many Haitian temples and have become coveted art items internationally. In the Haitian Creole language, these flags are called *drapo*. Traditionally, they measure approximately 3 square feet and can contain thousands of sequins. Flags to be used for ritual typically feature fringe around the edges. The flags are hand-sewn by Vodou initiates, with a prayer for the Lwa being said each time the needle passes through the sequin or the cloth. Working with the delicate process of creating these masterpieces teaches the Vodou initiate patience, respect, direction, and discipline. The process, like all in the religion, is a partnership between the individual and the Lwa. Dedication and single-mindedness are vital tools for psychic practitioners, for it is this type of intensity that the Lwa favor.

Members of the hounfor ceremonially promenade the flags as part of the opening calls of a Haitian Vodou ritual. Functioning as a focal point for the temple members, they allow the Lwa to manifest. During a ceremony, honored guests are sometimes permitted to walk underneath crossed pairs of flags. Sometimes the drapo depict images of the saints or the vévé for the Lwa. Like the ground vévés, they are used by the congregation's dancers and ritual participants to call the Lwa. They are seen as representations of the Lwa themselves on some level, having the ashé of the Lwa. The flags are kissed and danced with during ceremony, and great care is taken to make sure they are treated carefully and respectfully.

VODOU DRUMMING AND DANCE

Drums are an intrinsic part of any Vodou ritual or practice. They simultaneously focus and expand the power of the hounfor and the congregation. Ritual drumming involves a great deal of time and study. Some hounfor require drummers to learn upward of 50 different rhythms before they are considered worthy enough to play in ceremonies for the Lwa.

Haitian Vodou has three main drums that are played for rituals: the Maman, the Segunda (or Seconde), and the Petit or (Boulah). The Maman is the main ritual drum representing both Venus and the moon. The Segunda, the second drum, is for the energy of the Sun and Mars. The Petit, the smallest drum, is used to represent Mercury. The Gros Mambo who initiated me had a ritual drum that possessed the most beautiful ashé. The drum was ornately painted with vévés and other sacred symbols. The sound made your body and spirit travel swiftly back to Africa.

Fortunately, much of the information about ritual Vodou dances has been preserved by scholars such as Katherine Dunham, Maya Deren, and Zora Neale Hurston. All three women were pioneers in the study of Haitian Vodou during the 1930s and 1940s, received some form of initiation in the tradition, and were given access to many sacred rites and accompanying dances. Each of them separately shot film footage of the practices (this is discussed in more detail in chapter 10).

Dunham was a world-class dancer and choreographer who focused her early anthropological work on Haitian Vodou dances. According to her research, the dances she discovered in the Caribbean in 1937 were similar to ones described in the historical records of the 17th and 18th centuries. She studied in detail the rhythms and movements used for the Vodou Lwa. She found that often there was a complex connection at play, where dances were associated with rhythms, which were then in turn inconsistently applied to Lwa.

Deren was a Russian-born theorist and filmmaker who traveled to Haiti for the first time in 1947 to film ritual dances. Over the years, she became more and more involved with Vodou, and some reports even say she became a mambo dedicated to Erzulie. One of my favorite legends about her says that she was known for spontaneously succumbing to trance-possession at New York society cocktail parties. Deren was definitely a pioneering Vodou historian and filmmaker. Given that her theoretical work dealt with altering perceptions of time and space, it is easy to see how she became enthralled with Vodou's timelessness and transcendence. With regard to Vodou and dance, Deren noted the sacredness of small, repetitive movements. These movements are designed to induce and welcome trance-possession by the Lwa. Even the smallest repetitive movement can bring about a heightened state of consciousness for worshippers.

Deren was also one of the first Vodou scholars to discuss the strong connection between the dancers and the drummers. In the religion of Vodou, it is almost as if there is an astral cord running between the drummers and the dancers of the hounfor. Sacred feet are guided by sacred hands and vice versa.

There are several different Vodou ritual dances for the Lwa used to honor them during ceremony. Two of the most popular are the Yanvalou and the Banda. The Yanvalou is said to be danced to honor the serpent Damballa with a series of slow undulations and grinds. There is also a movement during the dance that was said to be used by the slaves as an encoded signal for revolt. It looks like a swift beheading and was most likely used to incite violence against the oppressors whenever the opportunity presented itself. This rhythm has also been attributed to the Lwa Maman Brigitte. It is frequently in three-quarter time and is favored among practitioners throughout the Caribbean and New Orleans.

Dancing in Congo Square. 1886 illustration depicting slave dances in New Orleans 40 some years earlier. – [public domain]

The Banda is performed for the ancestors. It is believed to be of Martinique and West African origin. Used at both funerals and rituals for the Barons and the Gede, the dance involves a series of grinds and low hip movements as the tempo builds to a climax.

The Kalenda, or Calinda, and the Bamboula are often described as socio-religious dances. In addition to these dances for each of the Lwa, there are also ones for each different nanchon, including Ibo, Congo, Petro, Fon, and others.

One beautiful example of Haitian dance occurs in the film *Stormy Weather*. Choreographed by Dunham, the dance accompanying the title song features a beautiful piece where the dancers whirl like a tornado to honor the ashé of the storm.

VODOU TRANCE-POSSESSION

The phenomenon of trance-possession is one that is often misunderstood in Western culture. Many people express fear and apprehension when confronted by the possibility of becoming a vehicle, or "horse," of the Lwa. There is no need for these feelings. Possession is a divine dance between an individual and a god. If we enter into the experience from a space of pure love, confidence, and trust, what will ensue is a beautiful blessing from the divine. Possession is a union, a true blessing from the spirits. By opening the links of pure energy, this allows us to become part oracle, part miracle worker, all divine. These trance-possessions grace our existence if we are fortunate. We should welcome the chance to become an instrument of the divine.

THE FEAST OF THE YAM

The Feast of the Yam in Haitian Vodou is celebrated each year during the month of October or November. It is a simple festival designed to honor the ancestors and thank them for a bountiful harvest. A large ritual bed is prepared with banana leaves, which are said to allow passage back to Africa. Participants may sit on the leaves while they are waiting for the yams to be prepared. Eventually, the yams are laid out on the leafy bed with candles and offerings of money. People eat and drink, and possessions by the Lwa and the ancestors occur well into the night. The festival can even stretch into a second day. The ceremony is meant to give back a portion of the bounty to the ancestors so they will continue to ensure the success of the descendants.

VODOU MAGICKAL ITEMS

Vodou is a religion replete with its own magickal tools and charms. These items serve as aids to attract and please the Lwa. There are tools that are only used by the mambo or the houngan, and tools that can be used by anyone. The most sacred tool for the mambo is the *asson*, which is a consecrated gourd rattle covered with beads and bones. It sometimes features snake vertebrae and a small bell. I've heard some say that it was originally decorated with the bones of one's enemy. The mambo and houngan use the asson to orchestrate the ritual. It is shaken to signal the drummers to change rhythms, to bless the congregation, or to call out for the Lwa. For some it comes as part of an initiation called the prise d'asson.

Each one of the Lwa also has sacred items that can be utilized by members of the congregation during ritual. These are things like Legba's cane or Ogou's machete. They help to assist with appeasing the Lwa. In many ways, this can add to the spectacle of the ceremony. There have even been a few times in ritual that I have lit a machete on fire, literally to strike a match to the ashé of Ogou.

Fire, however, is not the only way to create a spark, and the Paket Congo are the magickal spell bundles of Vodou that create their own type of heat. Dedicated to the Lwa, they are brightly decorated with sequins and feathers. The Paket Congo contain specific herbs and charms inside to help them bring about a desired result. Paket Congo can be created for healing, wealth, love, or any other purpose. The colors and ingredients used are appropriate for the specific Lwa. The bundles are wound around themselves with silk ribbons and fabric to contain and swaddle the magick inside. Believed to be created with the assistance of the ancestors, they work as guardian energies set to create magick. They can be created as part of an initiation or because a specific protection is needed.

VODOU CALENDAR

January 6—Marassa Feast Day for the divine twins of Vodou. Also the Day of the Kings Festival or Three Kings Day to change your fortune

March 16—Feast for Loko Davi, the Lwa of the center pole

April 31—Ancestor feasts for Les Morts (the dead)

June 24— Saint John's Eve holy day of ritual baths and blessings often in honor of Erzulie, the goddess of love

July 16—Sau D'Eau festival, which involves ritual baths in a waterfall for the Lwa Erzulie Freda and Damballa

July 25—Feast for Ogun, the god of war and technology

August 25—Feast for Damballa Wedo, the serpent creator of Vodou

November 1 and 2—Parties for the Gede, or unnamed ancestors

November 25—Mange Yam, or Feast of the Yams, a harvest festival

December 8—Festival to honor Aida Wedo, the wife of Damballa, for healing and love

December 10—Feast for Gran Bois, the Lwa of the forest

VODOU WORDS OF THE WISE

Damballa and Aida Wedo are the Lwa responsible for bringing the religion of Vodou across the sea and sky from Africa to the Americas. These divinities are envisioned as snakes. In serpent form, Damballa and Aida Wedo left Africa with the ancient knowledge of Vodou. Damballa took the route under the ocean, while Aida Wedo arched her serpent body across the sky to make the beautiful crown of the rainbow. They met on the island of Haiti, intertwining in an embrace of powerful love that gave birth to the Vodou religion.

The Marassa are the sacred twins of Haitian Vodou. Named Mawu and Lisa, they are the moon and the sun, a divine symmetry of the female and male energies of the cosmos. Together, they created the children of the world. According to legend, these two were separate at first, living on opposite sides of the sky, until one day there was an eclipse. They literally and figuratively came together and created seven pairs of twins. Twins are a blessing of great fortune throughout the African Diaspora, and these are the seven pairs of twin Lwa that started it all.

The twins of the earth were born first, followed by the twins of the sky—thunder and lightning. Next were the twins of iron, then the twins of the waters. Beasts had their own set of twins, as did the trees, and the final pair of twins were for the intermediate space between the earth and the sky. All the various sets of twins were told by Mawu and Lisa that they were to listen to and care for the humans, reporting back to Mawu and Lisa when necessary. This is why the Lwa are in the rivers, trees, and thunder, which surround everyone. The duality inherent in the divine twins makes possible not only the creation of opposites but also allows people to envision a way back to the divine.

VODOU BOTANICALS

The following is a partial list of the sacred herbs and plants used in Haitian Vodou:

Basile (*Basilique*)—Used for cleansing and exorcism

Bay laurel—Used to grant justice, guidance, and direction

Calabash gourd (*Calbasse*)—Used to hold other offerings for the Lwa

Cotton—Sacred to Damballa and Maman Brigitte; used to represent the silence that can speak volumes

Cornmeal (*Farine*)—Used for vévés

Mombin—Herb for purification

Palm—Sacred to Ayizan; used for cleansing and protection

Yam—Sacred food used to honor the ancestors

Almond tree—Susceptible to evil, so plant away from the house

Birch Gum tree—Used to get rid of enemies

Tobacco—Protection

Avocado—Healing

Banana—Knowledge, wisdom, peace

VODOU BEYOND THE SEAS

The future direction the Haitian Vodou practices will take is hard to predict. There is still the stronghold of devotion in both the country and urban centers like Port-au-Prince. Also, Vodou has increasingly become a tourist attraction in Haiti over the past 100 years. This has resulted in what I call "taxicab initiations." This is when tourists pay hundreds or thousands of dollars for a quick initiation into Vodou by someone opportunistic and most likely unqualified. The internet age has only intensified these issues. Ultimately, this jeopardizes the religion, which is based on powerful forces that require considerable training to work with. The economic reality in Haiti is certainly one of the root causes of these problematic practices. One can only hope that people will trust yet verify and be more careful and respectful in the future.

CHAPTER THREE

NEW ORLEANS VOODOO AND HOODOO

THE AMAZING AND THE OBSCURE

There is no official record of when the religion of Voodoo was introduced into North America, but most scholars agree it happened in New Orleans in the late 1700s. It is known that it made its way to the city in the hearts and minds of the slaves arriving from a variety of different locales: Africa, Guadeloupe, Martinique, and Santo Domingo. The 1809, migration alone brought over 6,000 Caribbean refugees to the city.

The history of Voodoo in New Orleans is an interesting one. It is peppered with exotic characters with names like Sanité Dédé, Marie Saloppé, Bayou John, Marie Laveau, Leafy Anderson, Lafcadio Hearn, and others. New Orleans has always been a city where fact mixes with fantasy, and the reality is that any reconstruction of these early days of Voodoo is difficult.

The earliest written historical record of a Voodoo priestess in New Orleans is Sanité Dédé, a free woman of mixed heritage from Santo Domingo. She is credited with operating a mixed-race Voodoo temple as early as 1822. An account of one of her ceremonies was published in the magazine *Century*. The report reputedly came from a teenage boy who claimed to have been led to the ceremony by one of his father's slaves. There, he witnessed a revelry of drumming, dancing, and trance-possession. It is said Dédé was a street food vendor, but there is no record of her in governmental or church records.

New Orleans, also known as the Crescent City, offers many Voodoo tales of the amazing and the obscure. Magick is always a combination of the tangible and the intangible, the physical and the ethereal. It operates in its own world, defying the need for logical explanation. The rituals of Marie Laveau, the most famous Louisiana Voodoo Queen, are no exception. Mademoiselle Marie lived from roughly 1794 or 1801, until 1881 (her birth year is heavily disputed among scholars). She was the first to dance with serpents during ritual. Her head covered in a *tignon* (headdress worn by Creole women in Louisiana), she carried her snake, Zombie, reputedly venomous, 20 feet long, fed on watermelon, and housed in an alabaster box. Laveau's ritual dance mimicked that of the snake: with her feet firmly planted on the ground, she turned and twisted and spun in the Louisiana air. Her power is the stuff of legend.

Baron vévé painting, Krewe du Vieux 2010. – [photo by author]

Laveau was the undisputed Voodoo Queen of New Orleans by the time she was 36 years old. She achieved her status due to a strong will, craft, and spirit. There is even the tale of Laveau's divination services being sought by Queen Victoria, and legend has her being visited by the Marquis de Lafayette. It is said that she thrived on publicity. One of the most fantastic tales surrounding her comes from her prison work, for which she was famous. In 1852, she is reported to have magickally postponed the executions of Jean Adam and Anthony Deslisle, who had been convicted of murdering a maid while robbing a house. On the bright and sunny day on which they were sentenced to die, she had brought them an intoxicating serving of Louisiana gumbo. As soon as they were led outside, the sky became dark and the wind began to howl. A thunderous storm came down, and when the men were placed in the nooses, the ropes broke and they plunged to the ground. The crowd mobbed the gallows. Unfortunately, the execution was only delayed 10 minutes. Everyone in attendance, however, attributed the strange occurrence to Laveau.

There are many different mythic tales surrounding Mademoiselle Marie. They include walking on water and her drowning and resurrection. Her talents were an omnipotent many, and her fame even more impressive. Her tomb is still a site of power and ritual and is visited more than any other grave in the United States except Elvis Presley's. Items from around her tomb, such as rocks, sticks, and the like, are reported to bring good fortune to those who come into contact with them. Unfortunately, the tomb was a site of vandalism over the years and is now only accessible with a licensed tour guide. Laveau's activities in the afterlife also continue in an unusual manner, with numerous sightings and events still being attributed to the great priestess.

The religion itself still thrives in the city as well, despite its status in many people's eyes as a simple tourist attraction. Drumming, dancing, and sacred ceremony are still a vital part of the New Orleans Voodoo experience. The historical record shows that public ritual dances were held there by slaves and free people of color in the 19th century, just as they are held today.

In New Orleans, a variety of both Lwa and Orisha are honored—the traditional ones from Haitian and Cuban pantheons, as well as ones visiting from other religious traditions like Hinduism and Buddhism. Louis Martinié of the Voodoo Spiritual Temple explains that "Voodoo takes on a form specific to place and time." Laveau's passion for serpents continues in the city, and gods and goddesses like Damballa and Aida Wedo, as well as Simbi, still thrive. Voodoo tours go throughout the French Quarter, and the more adventurous can go to the cemetery to leave an offering for Laveau, or dance the Bamboula in Congo Square, which is now part of Louis Armstrong Park. Ceremonies and drum circles are still held here weekly.

Some divinities are unique manifestations in the New Orleans area. The first of these is Papa Lebat.

THE LWA

Papa Lebat

Functioning in a similar capacity as Legba or Elegguá, this Lwa is invoked at the start of every ritual. He receives his name from the missionary Father Jean Baptiste Lebat. In the late 17th and early 18th centuries, Lebat was responsible for challenging the religion and trying to eradicate it. In typical Voodoo logic, he is given the responsibility for the opposite function that he performed in the physical world. This way, followers can use his name to their own advantage. Practitioners beg Papa Lebat to open the way, to open the gate for them to travel and serve. In some spiritual houses, Lebat can be called Limba or La Bas, as variation is the rule in the city.

Annie Christmas

Annie Christmas also seems to be a Lwa unique to the New Orleans area. Surviving mainly through folktales and myth, her fierce protection is the stuff of well-known legends. She is seen as a female incarnation of Ogou. The stories surrounding her tell of her being a railroad worker or a steamboat engineer in old New Orleans. She is honored with the clanging of metal and is offered traditional Ogou-type foods and beverages, such as undercooked meat and rum.

Ogou

The Haitian and African versions of Ogou are also honored here. Louis Martinié, coauthor of the *New Orleans Voodoo Tarot*, is a master of magickal waters. One of his preparations for Ogou involves making an Ogou Iron Stew with rusty metal gathered from the woods, nails, a hammerhead, and any other found pieces of iron. This can then be used as an offering for Ogou ceremonies.

LaSirene

LaSirene also finds a place in this watery city. Particularly revered by Mambo Sallie Ann Glassman, coauthor of the *New Orleans Voodoo Tarot*, this Lwa of the sea is an enchantress. She blesses the congregation with the gift of music and song. She is frequently given offerings of shrimp, champagne, seaweed, and seawater.

Mami Water

Mami Water, or Mami Wata, the Yoruba deity, also makes a reappearance in the New Orleans spiritual lineage. She is sung sweet songs and thanked for her nurturing maternal guidance. Priestess Miriam of the Voodoo Spiritual Temple once did an invocation to her to bless the sprinkling of rain that nourishes the earth.

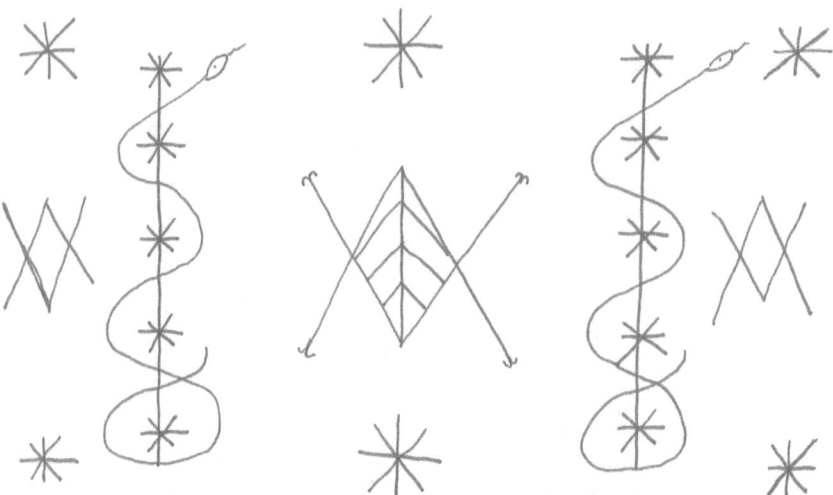

Ayizan vévé, also includes vévés for Damballa and the Marassa. [image by Tehron Gillis]

Ayizan

The canon is graced by the presence of the Lwa Ayizan. Evocative of the energy of the mambo of the temple, she represents love and deep levels of initiation. She teaches her children the joys of devotion. Ayizan is usually represented with the color pink and is offered sugarcane syrup, yams, and plantains. She has a special association with palm fronds, and I frequently see practitioners gathering these on Palm Sunday to use as a blessing for her. She is said to be the wife of Papa Loko, the guardian of the temple, and as such is a grounding and supportive force for the whole community.

Madame LaLune

Madame LaLune is the goddess of the moon. This Lwa is offered rice cakes, croissants, and half-moon cookies. She represents the mysteries of the unknown. The freezing plains of the moon, piercing and powerful, are at play here.

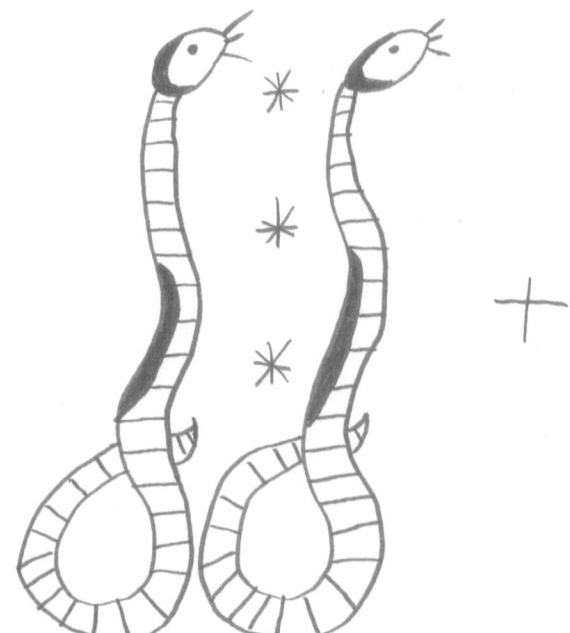

Damballa and Aida Wedo vévé. [image by Tehron Gillis]

Damballa and Aida Wedo

Even though they are not unique to the New Orleans area, the serpent gods Damballa and Aida Wedo are worshipped here to celebrate universal balance. Both my personal snake and the snake at the Voodoo Spiritual Temple were named in honor of the goddess Aida Wedo. Offerings for this divinity in New Orleans often take the form of cornmeal, powdered doughnuts, candy-covered almonds, milk, eggs painted in rainbow colors, and other typical Haitian offerings.

Oshún and Erzulie

Multi-traditional synthesis occurs here in New Orleans with practitioners and practices from all over the globe. There is frequently an incorporation of Celtic, Egyptian, Buddhist, Strega, Hindu, or Baptist practices. It's like a spiritual gumbo. Here, sometimes different versions of the same ashé are honored, as is the case with Oshún and Erzulie Freda Dahomey. An argument could be made that both of these energies are representative of the same function: love. New Orleans, however, makes a strong distinction is between the two realms. Erzulie Freda is the Lwa crying for the world that always disappoints her. Men and humanity never live up to her expectations, so she becomes frequently weighed down with this knowledge and is consumed by waves of tears. Oshún, however—often featured with a crying aspect in Yoruba theology and Santería practice—is given over to pure sensuality. She knows her hips generate both thought and action, and she loves it. The epitome of sensual love and ever-important desire, she is very often included in ceremony.

The Ancestors

The Crescent City sits below sea level, and the aura of the dead seeps through everything in it. There is a ritual focus on healing and ceremonies replete with drumming and dance. The Voodoo Spiritual Temple, of which I am a member, performs ceremonies for the ancestors each year. Priest Oswan Chamani passed on into the world of the "invisibles" in 1995. The temple continues to honor him as part of its own ancestral lineage, along with other temple members who are on the other side.

Ancestor spirits have always been strong in the region, as the aboveground dead are easily heard. Practitioners make regular visits to the cemetery to leave offerings of food, flowers, alcohol, and words of thanks. Oyá, the Santería mistress of the cemetery, is also given a place of prominence in the New Orleans religion. Oyá is offered eggplant, red wine, red or black grapes, and yams to show her connection to Africa, plus the traditional New Orleans dish of Red Beans and Rice.

For a time, the New Orleans Voodoo Museum even had its own Ghost Gallery, showcasing photographic manifestations of spirit. I participated in the dedication ceremony of the short-lived gallery in 2000. There, several

Lwa of the dead were honored—the Barons, the Gede, Oyá, and Maman Brigitte, just to name a few.

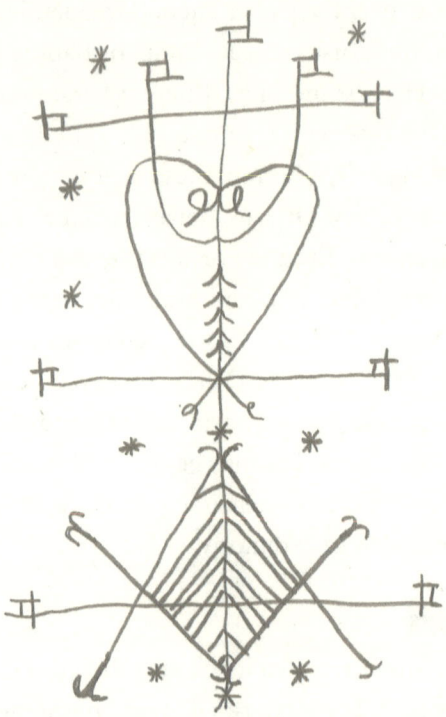

Maman Brigitte vévé in New Orleans voodoo. [image by Tehron Gillis]

HOODOO

The practices that are most often grouped together under Hoodoo have been described as everything from devout religion to complete hoax. In recent years, however, it has seen a resurgence and is beginning to get the recognition it deserves. The most formalized types of the religion occurred in Louisiana and South Carolina. Much research has been done in this area by pioneering Black anthropologist Zora Neale Hurston, who is better known for her novels and contribution to the Harlem Renaissance. Hoodoo involves the use of herbal and animal medicines and magick to bring about practitioners' desired results. Its followers often set up shop to offer cures and curses. Often, they refer to themselves as root doctors or two-headed men and women. The two heads refer to the fact that they are believed to have the power to see into both the physical and the spirit worlds. These practitioners also frequently operate as independent entities, running a one-person business to support the need in the area. The Hoodoo doctors are said to always have one hand, eye, or foot in both worlds: the visible and the invisible.

Dr. John was the most famous drummer in New Orleans history. Much scholarship has been done in this area since the first printing of this book. Records from the time are incomplete, but he most likely lived from 1801 to 1885. His real name was John Montanee (also spelled Montane and Montancé), and he hailed from Africa, most likely Senegal. Dr. John was said to be a root doctor, a conjure man, a real estate mogul, a "coffeehouse" owner, and was even reported in one census as a "quack." In reality, the Hoodoo practitioners of the southern United States created herbal concoctions that met a vital shortage in the rural communities with little or no access to health care. The preparations most likely provided the users with a sense of empowerment over their lives, which were often plagued with difficulties regarding the law, healing, finances, and love.

Hoodoo solutions were offered for just about every problem from an unfaithful mate to stolen livestock. The herbs and items used in traditional Hoodoo magick ran the gamut from the mundane to the bizarre. Often, practitioners could be found using Little John or the herb galangal for court cases and justice; tonka beans for gambling luck and wishes; graveyard dirt for curses and honoring the ancestral realm; Red Brick Dust for protection; raccoon penis bones for virility and potency; and black cat bones for power. The most popular "herb" by far was Hi John the Conqueror root. To obtain the maximum results from this root, it is customary to "fix," or prepare, it for magickal use, either as a pocket piece to carry or in a mojo bag. The following are two of the many ways a Hi John the Conqueror root can be fixed for magick:

·» To Draw Money

Wrap a bill by folding it around the Hi John the Conqueror root and keep it in your pocket (some people use nutmeg in the same manner). Anoint the root or the bill regularly with Hi John the Conqueror oil.

The higher the denomination of the bill, the more successful the charm will be.

⋙ Leap Into Money Working

Wrap a Hi John the Conqueror root and a silver dime in a $2 bill, folding the bill toward you, not away from you. If the dime and the bill have leap-year dates, all the better. Fix in a red or green mojo bag, usually flannel, and anoint with Money Drawing oil. Wear it when playing the lottery or betting, or place it near the door of your place of business to draw money to you through personal power.

Several of these Hoodoo-derived practices are still employed in New Orleans and throughout the rest of the southern United States.

⋙ THE SAINTS COME MARCHING IN ⋘
THE SYNCRETIZED SPIRITS OF NEW ORLEANS

Many of the traditional Voodoo and Hoodoo practices in New Orleans contain elements of Christianity. Followers frequently engage in bibliomancy, or divination with the Bible, and rely on saints and psalms as part of their rituals. The saints are prayed to for assistance with difficult situations, and psalms are used as magickal incantations and repeated during ritual workings. I remember the first time I attended a ceremony where someone became possessed by Jesus. To say the least, I was shocked and surprised. Then I learned from the houngan that this was a somewhat-frequent occurrence. He explained that Jesus does not behave like the Lwa during possession: sometimes it can be difficult to convince him to leave, as he often wishes to give a sermon.

A variety of practices are always in an eclectic chorus in the Hoodoo and Voodoo traditions. Real Catholic saints and made-up ones grace the list of those worshipped in New Orleans Voodoo. The saints are turned to for every sort of problem:

Saint Peter

Saint Peter with his keys helps people unlock tricky situations. But be careful because he is said to be an unruly saint who can punish just as fast as he can bless.

Saint Anthony

Saint Anthony is to be hung inside the house, behind the front door, to guide the faith inside. He is also helpful for those who have lost something.

Saint Raymond

Saint Raymond is the saint to petition when you need to keep the law away.

Saint Joseph

Saint Joseph has been celebrated vigorously in New Orleans for the past 200 years. It is both a holiday for Catholics, who create elaborate altars and feasts to salute this saint who keeps famine away, and also for the Mardi Gras Indians, who regard this as a high point of the year, coming out in full costume and fanfare.

Saint Expedite

Saint Expedite is by far the most popular saint. In reality, he isn't a saint at all. His name comes from packages that were stamped "Expedite" by the U.S. Postal Service. Practitioners noted that this word was an effective type of magick and began praying to Saint Expedite. Candles and oils for this speedy and effective saint can be found in most botanicas or religious supply shops.

Saint Rita

Saint Rita is the divine lady who gives assistance to women who are suffering from domestic violence. If this is your problem, please seek help immediately from your local domestic-violence hotline. It is said that the saint was a woman abused by her husband for 18 years before he died, after which she joined the convent. Saint Rita is said to be present when roses bloom out of season.

Saint Marta

Saint Marta is revered in New Orleans as the patron of drummers. She is powerful and swift in her actions. Often, she is pictured with snakes or a three-toed mythic dragon. She is invoked by women seeking a husband.

Saint Dymphna

Saint Dymphna is the patron saint of the mentally ill and those about to have a nervous breakdown. Like Saint Rita, Dymphna was abused by a family member; specifically, she was murdered by her father. Dymphna offers devotees strength through what can seem like impossible difficulty.

Mary Magdalene

Mary Magdalene is honored in New Orleans Voodoo by sex workers and by women who have relationship troubles in general. Her sacred sexuality is worshipped and enlisted by devotees.

Saint Martin DePorres

Saint Martin DePorres fights against racial injustice; as such, he is held in a special place in the hearts of the African American followers of Voodoo. He is frequently associated with the Orisha Changó and is also revered by Peruvians.

Our Lady of Prompt Succor

Our Lady of Prompt Succor has, in recent times, become central in celebrations in the city to protect the residents from storms.

Saint Anne

Saint Anne is the patroness of grandmothers (as she was Jesus' grandmother), housewives, and mothers. She is used by some to find a male partner by praying, "Saint Anne, Saint Anne, I need a man."

Saint Paul

Saint Paul is often depicted wielding a sword. As a patron of writers and journalists, he is afforded a place of honor in this city that was at one time home to literary greats like Tennessee Williams and Charles Bukowski.

DIVINATION

In New Orleans Voodoo, there are both traditional and non-traditional types of divination. Priest Louis Martinié of the Voodoo Spiritual Temple and Mambo Sallie Ann Glassman of the Island of Salvation Botanica are the coauthors of the *New Orleans Voodoo Tarot*. The deck functions as a great tool for both divination and meditation and is used throughout the New Orleans and larger Voodoo community. In addition to cards, Voodoo practitioners also use palmistry, geomancy (with bones and semiprecious stones), astrology, and other forms of divination. Regular consultations are scheduled to deal with all aspects of one's life. In other forms of African Traditional Religion, practitioners also rely heavily on divination conducted with specific shells and nuts. Devotees receive a reading daily or weekly to be sure they are receiving proper guidance and are on the correct path to ensure their success.

THE ART
OF NEW ORLEANS VOODOO AND HOODOO

The art of the Hoodoo and Voodoo practices of the southern United States is a mixed bag. Both traditional and iconoclastic are present here. Artists such as Twafey, Sallie Ann Glassman, Mahalia Stines, Nema, and Charles Gandolfo take the classic form of the Haitian vévé and expand on it in their own work. Nema's interpretation of the Erzulie vévé as the breathing heart hangs in the Voodoo Spiritual Temple in New Orleans as part of the Erzulie shrine there.

THE MUSIC
OF NEW ORLEANS VOODOO AND HOODOO

Music is inseparable from the image of the city of New Orleans. Blues, jazz, and zydeco all sing their songs here. Places like the extremely raunchy neighborhood of Storyville saw Voodoo and jazz rise up side by side.

Many blues songs directly tell about Hoodoo and its practices, underscoring its importance. Blues, jazz, Voodoo, and Hoodoo are all mistakenly associated with the devil. The Hoodoo devil does not, however, embody evil as the Christian concept would like us to observe it. This devil, also described as "the rider" or "big black man," opens your roadways and bestows talent in any area you request it, be it musical prowess, gambling success, or gold strikes.

There is an infamous legend about the guitarist Robert Johnson, the greatest bluesman ever, selling his soul to the devil at the crossroads at midnight. Johnson was born in Mississippi in 1911 and, supposedly, had always been a mediocre musician. After the deaths of his wife and baby, he took a hiatus from the blues circuit in the early 1930s. When he returned a master guitarist, rumors began to circulate. Supposedly, he filed his fingernails all the way down to the quick and traded guitars with the devil. People said he sold his soul to the devil for this newfound musical talent. There is no real evidence that any satanic worship was going on. Most likely, Johnson, who was famous for singing about Hoodoo "mojo" and "hot-foot powder," had made an offering to Papa Lebat (or Legba) at the crossroads. Legba's sacred times of day are midnight and noon. In between times, these moments stand on the edge, just like Legba stands on the edge between the world of humanity and the world of the Lwa. Johnson went on to become a historic blues figure, and the story has continued ever since.

The jazz great Louis Armstrong is synonymous with the city of New Orleans, and his association with Hoodoo and Voodoo is a natural consequence. Armstrong is treated as a revered ancestor spirit in the religions. The park that houses Congo Square, where the sacred rites of Voodoo have been practiced for over 100 years, has been renamed Louis Armstrong Park. A statue of Armstrong greets people as they enter the gates. These are the gates where police once stood in a vain attempt to intimidate Marie Laveau, the great Voodoo Queen, and force her to cease her rituals. Practitioners leave offerings in this park to honor Armstrong and all the magick that has happened there.

The passing of Ray Charles was felt deeply by the city of New Orleans. At the time of his death, there were several "second line" festivities for him, where people go through the streets playing jazz music and parading. These ceremonies are held for funerals, weddings, births, and other occasions.

Many were moved by Charles and felt they needed to honor him when he crossed over into the land of the ancestors. Voodoo practitioners will add him to the list of honored dead, and maybe someday people will dance on a vévé of sunglasses and a big smile for Ray Charles.

THE MAGICKAL ITEMS
OF NEW ORLEANS VOODOO AND HOODOO

The bulk of the philosophy of New Orleans Voodoo and Hoodoo is based on the principle that everyone and everything possesses divine ashé. Consequently, some of the most unusual people and things receive honor and sacred significance in the religions. One Voodoo Temple even has a disco ball hanging up to honor the Lwa. This illustrates the principle that everyone needs to have fun, even the Lwa.

New Orleans is a large city that, like most large cities, has a serious homelessness crisis. Yet here, these homeless are given special consideration. They are viewed as messengers of the divine and, as such, are able to confer special blessings. Voodoo followers anxiously wait to run into the "Bead Lady" or the "Herb Guy" on his bike. Some, like "Chicken Man," have continued to generate legends long after their death. These individuals are, even though they have almost nothing materially, given the deference and respect that everyone deserves. Items obtained from them are said to have great ashé.

Elaborate masks are another element of the New Orleans Voodoo tradition. The masks of Voodoo very often pay homage to the Mardi Gras Indians, a form of Mardi Gras krewe, or organization, made up of mostly inner-city Blacks, many of whom have native and/or maroon heritage. The name Mardi Gras Indians was taken to pay respect to the indigenous Louisiana tribes who assisted escaping enslaved people. The creation and wearing of these costumes is referred to as masking. The Mardi Gras Indian masks and headdresses are also used in Voodoo to salute the tradition, which has been in place for well over 100 years.

For the past 20 years, Sunpie Barnes and the North Side Skull and Bone Gang have kept alive a 200-year-old tradition of masking skeleton on Mardi Gras morning. With drummers, stilt walkers, and dancers, they travel through the Treme neighborhood saluting those who have gone before and those to come with music, dance, and fun.

Both Voodoo and the Mardi Gras Indians pay tribute to the spirit of Black Hawk, who was a 19th-century Native American. He fought valiantly to get his tribal land back from the U.S. government and the white settlers. Even Abraham Lincoln was part of the militia that sought to find and capture Black Hawk. He was eventually defeated at Bad Axe on the Mississippi River. For Voodoo practitioners, Black Hawk represents the fight for racial justice. Individuals light candles and leave offerings of sage, tobacco, feathers, and animal bones. The population of New Orleans is overwhelmingly made up of people of color, so the importance of racial equality is always evident. Sacred masks like the ones worn by the Mardi Gras Indians remind practitioners that sometimes one's face needs to be hidden to challenge the enemy.

The *irukere*, or bull tail whip, is another sacred item used in Voodoo. It is consecrated to Oyá and, on rare occasions, to Obatalá. During a ritual, the whip is used to keep spiritual currents in line. It is presented to the cardinal points and then used to bless participants. The ashé of the Lwa, Orisha, and the ancestors is focused through the use of the whip.

THE CALENDAR
OF NEW ORLEANS VOODOO AND HOODOO

Mardi Gras (the day before Ash Wednesday). North Side Skull and Bone Gang celebration at dawn.

January 8 – Feast of Our Lady of Prompt Succor. Offerings are made to protect the city from hurricanes.

March 19 – Saint Joseph's Day. Feasts and altars are created to stave off famine, and Mardi Gras Indians celebrate their tradition in all their finery.

May 15 – Saint Dymphna's Feast Day. This is the day of her martyrdom.

June 23—Saint John's Eve. Both Saint John's Eve and Saint John's Day, June 24, have been celebrated in New Orleans since colonial times. For Voodoo practitioners in the city, the day is celebrated as one of the longest in the year. It is a time of cleansing and healing.

THE MYTHOLOGY
OF NEW ORLEANS VOODOO AND HOODOO

In a city famous for its drumming and storms, it is no wonder that the deities Changó, lord of thunder and drumming, and Oyá, mistress of lightning and the storm, hold a special place in the hearts of Voodoo practitioners here. The following is a tale about how thunder and lightning came to fight side by side in battle.

> *The lord Changó was once a king and, as such, fought many bitter and difficult wars. Courageous and brave, Changó would mount his steed and ride into battle. After one particularly long and unsuccessful fight, Changó found himself cornered in the forest. He used his last bit of strength to escape to his wife Oyá's home in the middle of the woods. Too weak to continue the fight, he asked for her help. She asked why he only came around when he needed help. Changó explained he was hurt and needed to find a way to escape for a while and recuperate. Oyá, the ashé of lightning and wind, soon came up with a cunning plan. She told him that when night came, he was to put on her dress. When the sun set, she cut off her hair and weaved it into Changó's hair. Walking into the night, he made it past the enemy camps without incident. After he had rested for a few days, Changó began his assault again. Still wearing Oyá's clothes and hair, he confounded his opponents, who believed Oyá had used her powers to turn into Changó. They believed this until Oyá joined her husband in battle, slaughtering and screaming. The couple was victorious, and ever since they have fought side by side, with Changó being the ashé of thunder and Oyá the ashé of lightning.*

THE BOTANICALS
OF NEW ORLEANS VOODOO AND HOODOO

Basil—Healing and exorcism

Camphor—Cleansing and banishing

Chicory—For the ancestors

Copal—Healing and happiness

Cypress—Protection and to know secrets

Fig—To cause illness

Five-Finger Grass—Money, happiness

Frankincense—Blessing

Geranium—Legal problems

Hi John the Conqueror Root—Wealth, justice, happiness

Hyssop—Protection

Jalop—Success

Jasmine—Money and love

Lavender—All-purpose herb

Lemon balm—Love and joy

Lemon verbena—Love

Lodestone—Gambling and financial luck

Myrrh—Healing, cleansing, protection, to change one's luck

Myrtle—Love

Olive oil—Healing, knowledge

Patchouli—Love and passion

Saint John's Wort—Healing, luck

Sassafras—To gain the assistance of your ancestors

Sesame seeds—Money, exorcism, protection from death

Spanish moss—Spiritual power, protection by ancestors

Spearmint—Success

Staff of Dr. John. - [photo by author]

⁂ EXTEND YOURSELF ⁂

New Orleans Voodoo and Hoodoo have always been all-inclusive traditions. If something works, practitioners will try it here. The religions are constantly changing, expanding, and incorporating new elements. When

I received the New Year's blessing from the Voodoo Spiritual Temple, it spoke of extending oneself—extending both one's body and mind to new realms, to perceive new concepts and energies that may further the tradition. In my lifetime I have already seen ever-increasing success and popularity brought to the religion, and I hope it will continue to do so in a respectful way.

CHAPTER FOUR
SANTERÍA
THE RULE OF THE DIVINE

One of the most formal variations of African-derived religion can be found when examining the beliefs and practices of Santería. The proper name for the religion is Regla de Ocha, which roughly translates from Spanish to "rule of the divine," or Lucumí, an Afro-Cuban word for describing those religious practices that are derived from the Yoruba of West Africa. In this religion, tradition is paramount: The practices of the religion were brought with the slaves and, since that time, an emphasis on the importance of the proper way of conducting the practices has never left the people. However, modern times have seen police brutality, rising violence against women, and many other problems. Until the recent political unrest in Nigeria and other parts of Western Africa, many Lucumí devotees would travel back to the area to make sure their religious beliefs are in keeping with the spiritual motherland. This has become increasingly difficult.

Lucumí divinities are called Orisha. They are numerous, with counts sometimes running as high as 401 different Orisha—the number 401 being presumed to stand for as many as an individual can think of (400), and then add one more. They each have their own colors, ritual days for worship and offerings, feast days, *elekes* (ritual necklaces), herbs, foods, drinks, and saints that were used to depict the Orisha when more traditional African-looking images were prohibited.

ORISHA

Olorun

Leading the way in the pantheon, the one supreme god (for lack of a better term) is Olorun. Some believe this to be the same as Olodumare or Olofin, so this Orisha is seen as a supreme being, represented by the dove. Olorun does not typically manifest in trance-possession during ceremonies, and no typical sacrifices or offerings are made to this energy. This original god is said to quietly preside over all actions.

Elegguá, the trickster Orisha of the crossroads. – [Adobe stock]

Elegguá

Elegguá, or Elegua, is the trickster Orisha of the crossroads. Similar to Eshú, he is responsible for opening people's paths and providing a means of communication between humans and gods. The colors associated with him are usually red and black. His number is 3 or 21, the latter usually referring to the number of paths or avatars he has. He teaches those wise enough to listen to him the lessons of humility. Elegguá's cryptic guidance is the stuff of legend. He speaks in riddles and is always difficult to understand.

His colors and his mischievous ways have often found him misinterpreted as a type of devil. Elegguá is like a little troublemaker, always mischievous, stealing, and laughing. Prayers for him ask his assistance in opening doors, roads, and paths, and also closing them. Not all magick calls for opening things up; sometimes opposing forces need to be shut down for real progress to occur. In La Regla Lucumí, Elegguá is consulted frequently through divination so worshippers know which course of action to take.

Elegguá is traditionally represented with a coconut, a cement head with cowrie-shell eyes, or a stone. This head is filled with various ritual herbs and magickal items. He is often equated with the image of Saint Anthony, the Infant of Atocha, and the lonely soul, or anima sola. Occasionally, the Catholic image of Saint Anthony or Saint Peter is also featured. The physical items are often embellished. I received a coconut from one Santera (priestess) that was shaved and painted half-red and half-black. Several Elegguá cement heads have been adorned with hats and other head coverings. Like the Yoruba Eshú figures, they almost all feature some kind of blade or nail coming out of the head.

Ogún

Along with Elegguá, Ogún and Ochosi form the trinity called the Warriors. These three travel together and are often referred to as brothers. Together, the three open our path, cut away the brush, and guide us down the road. Without their assistance, no real action can take place on either the physical or spiritual realm.

Ogún is the ashé of iron and the white-hot forge. An ancient Orisha, he is the patron of blacksmiths and is also responsible for war, healing, and technology. He is believed to symbolize the place he is said to inhabit: the forest. He spends much of his time in isolation, working on his craft. His solitude should not necessarily be read as loneliness but as an exclusionary devotion to the task at hand. In addition to the forest, Ogún's abodes in the Santería tradition are the railroad tracks, the hospital, the internet, and the gun rack.

In some houses, he is offered a special kind of rum called *chamba*, which is infused with several different types of hot peppers and, occasionally, gunpowder. It is often used to test a person's possession experience, as only a true manifestation of Ogún could take a healthy swig of chamba. Modern times have transformed him into the patron of not only blacksmiths but also healers, the military, police officers, firefighters, engineers, and people who work with automobiles and computers. He is the divinity that sanctions all sacrifice, and all ritual knives, machetes, chains, hammers, and shovels are his domain. He is in charge of the ritual cutting of initiates that takes place in some iles. He therefore cuts the flesh of both animals and initiates. He is not to be angered under any circumstances; it is said of him that if he really likes you, "he only takes a limb." Ogún is often represented on ritual shrines with an iron cauldron.

The Orisha Ogún is represented in this tradition with the colors green and black. His altar is required to have at least two pieces of iron, as the Orisha resides in the ashé of the metal. Chains, tools, knives, and other weapons are all at home on his shrine.

Ochosi

Ochosi is the Orisha of the hunt, jails, and spiritual direction. This Orisha teaches devotees the lesson that the best path to their destiny is not always the straightest one. There is an aspect of Ochosi that deals with astral travel. It is under this cover that Ochosi teaches us to unify our heads and our hearts, thereby transcending time and space to bring us closer to our true path. Traditional Ochosi societies in Africa consisted of the hunters and trackers responsible for providing sustenance for the community. Thus, one of the favorite chants for him translates as, "Ochosi makes the hunger run." This speaks to his abilities as a lifesaving hunter and provider. In true ironic fashion, he is said to be a finicky eater, and he is often offered smoked fish, possum, venison, and a variety of herbs. Ochosi's preferred beverage is anisette, and his ritual number is 7. The ritual possession dance done for him mimes his hunting prowess, as initiates often seem to be stalking, aiming, and shooting an arrow.

He is said to originate from Ketu in West Africa. But many of the original societies honoring him were captured and transported to this country as enslaved people. Because of his association with the forest, he was connected to the Native Americans in the new land. Many Native Americans had frequent contact with the transplanted African communities. This was especially true of the Seminole tribes in Florida. Zora Neale Hurston, the pioneering African American anthropologist, came from Eatonville, Florida, the nation's first all-Black incorporated town. My paternal grandfather came from the same area of the state. Here, the

Seminole people lived, worked, loved, and played with the large African American population. The connection with the indigenous magick and the hunting magick of the transplanted Africans was most likely similar. The affinity between the two groups has continued in the practices for Ochosi.

Given that Ochosi is the owner of jails, followers often offer him a small jail cell for his shrine with the prayer, "Ochosi, please come and live in my house so I do not have to live in yours." Ochosi, the hunter and provider, has an altar decorated with items that reflect his favorites, such as animal skins, antlers, and turquoise to reinforce his connection to indigenous peoples; a bow and arrow, and scales representing justice, and even small jails. His colors can be green, black, blue, or peach.

Obatalá

There are, indeed, many other Orisha honored within the tradition. Leading the group on the earthly plane is Obatalá. This Orisha is the androgynous father and mother of peace and purity. They are the ashé of the clouds. Their ritual symbols are the elephant, the snail, the dove, silver, and cotton. Their clothes and other items are usually pure white as the progenitor of both the planet and peace. Cleanliness is also important to Obatalá. Usually, the practitioner will clean with regular mundane cleaning products and then do a wash or a sprinkling of holy water. Obatalá's ritual tools are usually crafted of silver, and they are also known to use a white irukere. Obatalá is the divine potter and sculptor responsible for crafting the world. This Orisha never takes any alcohol, and there is a mythological basis for this. One mythical story tells of how they became inebriated, and while creating people they lost focus, causing some to be deformed. It is said that children of Obatalá "can't have a drink, only a drunk," meaning they are incapable of responsible drinking. In addition to the drinking prohibition, Obatalá's devotees are not allowed to be naked in front of anyone or use foul language. Some practitioners even speak their words through cotton so the prayer will be purified before being sent to Obatalá. The ceremonial day for Obatalá is Sunday. On this day, practitioners make offerings of cool rainwater, white yams, and other white foods. In control of the head and, therefore, the destiny of all the practitioners, Obatalá is turned to for calm and mediation. Sometimes practitioners will wrap their heads in *cascarilla*, or powdered eggshell, covering it with white cloth to bring Obatalá's purity to their heads. Images of the Virgin of Mercy are frequently associated with La Regla Lucumí altars for Obatalá. The items one would usually find there are a sun, moon, an elephant or snail, and a silver snake.

Orunmilá

The deity responsible for the energy of divination is called Orunmilá, Ifá, or Orunla. Associated with Saint Francis, this deity is petitioned frequently in times when indecision causes the practitioner to lose his or her way. As I have mentioned, adherents to the religion consult divination frequently, and this process is mediated through babalawos dedicated to Orunmilá.

Altar to Yemaya. – [photo by author]

Yemaya

Yemaya is the mother of the ocean, the sea queen, the divine womb of creation. Legend says she possesses powers of divination that she either learned or took from her lover, Orunla. There are also numerous stories about her bestowing gracious gifts from the sea. Seen as the sister of Oshún and the mother of several other Orisha, she plays a key part in the familial structure of the pantheon. Described as dark and radiant, this Orisha is traditionally offered watermelon, cantaloupe, sugarcane syrup, gin, molasses, candy, blue stones like sodalite or lapis, seawater, seashells, and other items from the ocean. She is often represented by a statue or image of Diosa el Mar. Yemaya's ritual number is 7. Yemaya is gentle with her children and is often appealed to for peace and calm. Always compassionate, she kindly listens to all their problems and does her best to wash them away. Her counterpart is Olokun, the ashé of the depths of the ocean. Seen occasionally as male and other times as female, only Olokun knows what lies at the bottom of the ocean.

Yemaya is associated with a plethora of fish imagery, as well as dolphins, shells, sea glass, and other items connected with the sea. Her colors are blue and white. Shrines dedicated to her feature lace and satin, often with a length of the cloth draped over them like a canopy. Since her number is 7, shells or coins are sometimes given in multiples of seven.

Oshún

One of the most popular and honored of the Orisha is definitely Oshún. She is the ashé of the river. Her ritual candles and oils are always the first to float off the shelves at most botanicas. Her popularity is due, in a large part, to the fact that this beautiful, sensual goddess represents love, gold, fertility, and marriage. One of the three wives of the god Changó, she delights all with her sumptuous dances of love. At one time or another, Ogún, Elegguá, and Changó have all succumbed to the powers of Oshún's charms. With her celestial honey and her undulating hips, there are few who are immune to her devices. For women in Western society, sexuality and coquettishness are not always seen as strengths and virtues. Oshún teaches us that we need to explore and utilize all our strengths. It is then that we can shine in our full golden glory like the Orisha Oshún.

Described as always beautiful, she is a leader of women and the goddess of the Osun River in Nigeria. Her color (and metal) is gold. This Orisha is often represented with a peacock or buzzard. The buzzard is believed to represent her power to protect against evil. She adores yellow flowers, fans, mirrors, amber, honey (which must be tasted first to prove it is not poisoned), oranges, nutmeg, cinnamon, pumpkin (although, to some initiates, this food is a taboo), and sweet drinks. Oshún's number is 5, and offerings are frequently made in multiples of that number. She is said to wear five bracelets so you can always hear her coming. Petitioned with a small brass bell, Oshún possesses a strong magnetic force of attraction. Sometimes she is equated with the Virgin of Caridad del Cobre, the patron saint of Cuba. Popular legend has it that a statue of this virgin was found floating off the coast of El Cobre, a copper mining area. The virgin was placed in a church, and soon the statue miraculously disappeared. The location where it was discovered was where the devotees built their new church, which has remained on that site on and off throughout the years.

Oshún loves her peacock feathers and bells. All is to be golden, and frequently people cover the entire altar with gold glitter to increase its sparkle. Incidentally, this is also a technique used by some to fuse a candle with a particular Orisha's ashé. Mirrors, fans, jewelry, perfume, and makeup are also appropriate shrine offerings. Every offering for her represents the sacred power of sensuality. Her altar should be as pleasing to touch as it is to look at. Like Obatalá, she is demanding of cleanliness at all times.

Changó

Changó, or Shangó, is the lord of fire, passion, and the drum. A vital part of the religion, Changó infuses it with his pure masculine energy and fertility to bring it a full-bodied flavor. He is sometimes referred to as Changó Macho, as he is pure male sexuality; in fact, all his spiritual children are referred to as sons. He is also alternatively given the names Jakuta and Oba Koso, which refer to his status as king.

The pulse and rhythm of the drums are his. His charm and ego are legendary. Changó embodies the joy of life. He adores living and is said to be the only Orisha who never died. He is offered thunderstones (special stones believed to have been struck by lightning) and is said to have a healthy appetite for apples, bananas, cashews, patchouli, musk, pine, okra, steak, prairie oysters, dark beer, rum, red wine, and cigars (but do not smoke recreationally in his presence, as it is believed to offend him). His numbers are traditionally 4 or 6. In this branch of African Traditional Religion, he possesses a set of ritual tools called *ashé Changó*. They consist of six wooden (frequently cedar) tools, including a double-headed axe and a sword. He brings great luck, often in the form of gold and silver. He is said to be present in the sound of thunder and in the sideways red lightning that often occurs during a summer storm. He has three wives: Oyá, Obá, and Oshún. There are two Catholic images associated with him: Saint Barbara and a Black version called Barbara Africana. Some question the association of macho energy with a female saint. Saint Barbara is, in many ways, the logical choice, as she is dressed in Changó's ritual colors of red and white and carries a double-edged sword, with which he is said to administer justice.

Changó, the lord of the drum and dance, is one of the few Orisha who is represented by an African-looking image. In statue form, Changó is usually a Black man with African features, possessing either a drum (in some cases a set of drums) and/or a pile of jewels. Changó altars are washed in his ritual baths and decorated with opulent items of red. He is often honored on Friday or Saturday. The father of Changó is believed to be Aganyú.

Aganyú

The lord of the volcano, the ashé of explosive lava, is Aganyú, also called Agayu, Agayu Sola, and Agallu. He is the patron of travelers and is associated with Saint Christopher, who works for the same purpose. Red is the color for this god, who is traditionally offered bull horns in pairs to keep him happy. His ritual day is Wednesday, and he is customarily fed goats, green plantains, and roosters.

Oyá

Oyá is the goddess of the wind, the hurricane, the tornado, and change. She shoots her lightning ashé at her target to produce power and transformation. Oyá also possesses the ability to shapeshift, and there are many legends of her slipping into the skin of an animal and hiding in wait in the jungle to gain the advantage. She is also the master of interspecies communication.

Oyá is represented with lithographs of Saint Marta with the snakes or dragon, Saint Theresa with the bouquet of flowers, or Our Lady of Candlearia, often depicted as a Black Madonna. She is a fighting warrior of the highest order, riding in battle alongside her husband, Changó. Lightning sparks are said to shoot out from her hair, and she is said to have an excess of testosterone-like energy that gives her a beard whenever she has to do battle. Oyá can be seen as both stern and sexual. Her metal is copper, and some say her stone is sugalite or amethyst. Her number is 9, as she is said to have nine children. Indeed, her other name, Yansa, literally means "mother of nine." Oyá loves to garden, surrounding herself with flowers and spending time with the earth. As such, she is the Queen of all the ancestors. She is given eggplants, violets, red wine, red grapes, curry goat, plums, and dark rum. Her colors are purple and green, and her children are the only Orisha devotees allowed to wear dark colors. She is often depicted as masked, and certain legends say it is dangerous to look on her face. While the most frequent ritual images for the Orisha Oyá are Saint Marta and Saint Theresa, I was also told by a Santera that Our Lady of Candlearia can also be used to salute this windy goddess. The colors used are either black or purple, or sometimes even a rainbow. Due to her connection with nature, several plants and flowers, such as purple basil, carnations, and lilies, are also present.

Obá

Obá is the third wife of Changó. Always faithful and obedient, she is often represented by Saint Rita, the patron of hopeless cases. Obá is said to live in all lakes. The most popular story relating to her tells of the time she was tricked by Oshún. Obá, the kind and devoted wife of Changó, would do anything to make him happy. One day she saw his other wife, Oshún, preparing him his favorite soup. Desperate to please him as Oshún could, she asked for the recipe. Oshún would never give up her advantage over a man, so she quickly made up a recipe that was sure to anger the lord of fire and passion. She told Obá that the magick ingredient was her ears: she had to cut them off and place them in his soup to ensure his love. Obá quickly followed Oshún's instructions. Changó, upon his first taste, spit out the bad-tasting concoction. He realized what she had done and was filled with displeasure. Some say he never forgave her. Today, Obá occupies a somewhat marginal role in the tradition and, although I have heard people refer to her, there are choice few who identify themselves as devotees, or children, of Obá. Her color is pink, and she is fed goats and doves.

Babaluaiyε and Nana Buluku

Babaluaiye (Omolu) is the Orisha dedicated to curing infectious disease. Originally the god of smallpox and leprosy, his domain has now expanded to include HIV/AIDS, COVID-19 and other modern plagues. He is offered peas, beans, and popcorn. The ritual number ascribed to him is 17. He is said to travel in the company of his faithful dogs and is depicted as Saint Lazaro. He is often given crutches. Mosquitoes and flies are said to be his messengers as the carriers of many diseases.

Nana Buluku is another of the Orisha that is associated with both male and female energy. She is ancient and powerful. Her offerings include mint and yams.

Ibεji

The divine twins in the Santería pantheon are known as Ibeji, or Ibbeyi. The word is believed to translate from the two Yoruba root words: *Ibi*, which means "to give birth," and *eji*, which is representative of the number 2. The patron saints of all children, they are especially revered in the tradition. The Yoruba are said to have the highest incidence of twinning in the world, a unique and special blessing that is believed to be a sign of extreme luck. Some believe them to be the children of Oshún, while still other houses say they are the offspring of Oyá. All legends place them as the children of the Orisha Changó. Representative of both duality and perfect balance, they are honored throughout the tradition.

Osanyin

Osanyin, Osonyin, Osain, or Aroni, is the masterful lord of herbal medicine. He is equated with Saint John (San Jose) and Saint Ambrose, among others. His day of the week is Sunday. His priests are frequently ventriloquists. The wrought-iron bird staff is one of the most important symbols for Osanyin. The simplest version, called the *osun* staff or *orere*, is composed of a solitary iron bird sitting on an iron disk that surmounts several iron bells. It is said that this staff has the power to warn of upcoming death or of the *aje* (witches) and can also protect against insanity or other dislocations of reason. The many examples of these staffs are not only beautiful works of art in their own right but also serve as elaborate metaphors for the power of Osanyin to combat illness and sorcery.

One of the most distinguishing characteristics of Osanyin is his unusual appearance: He has one arm, one leg, one eye, and one of his ears is small and shriveled. These disadvantages are explained by several legends as his punishment for trying to keep all of the herbal knowledge to himself. The message is simple: sharing is imperative both for gods and men. Before any herb is taken for ritual, an offering must be made to Osanyin. Sharing all in the existential now is a lesson that everyone must learn—one way or another.

Inle

Inle is the Orisha of fisherpeople. He is adept at healing magick and the sciences. He is represented by Saint Rafael, and his day is Friday. His number is 7 or 24, and his color is deep-green, which is representative of seawater.

SANTERÍA DRUMMING AND DANCE

Sacred drums and dances occupy an important component in the religion. Drumming and dance are a part of every ceremony and often even find their way into secular celebrations as well. Members of a house are specifically trained in the rhythms and movements of each of the different Orisha. Drums are seen to represent the memory, the soul, and the liveliness of the temple. Most often, the drumming consists of a group of three drums called Bata. These are hourglass-shaped drums with a skin on both sides. Each drum is considered an honored guest at the ceremonies and is often covered with bells, clothes, and various ritual adornments. The largest drum is called the *iya*, or mother, the "next in line" is the *itotele*, followed by the *okonkolo*. Under the guidance of Changó, their creator, they bring the blessed rhythms to the entire congregation.

The most common drum ceremony performed in Santería is a bembe, or tambor. Simply a drum and dance ceremony appropriate for several different occasions, these take place frequently for the Orisha feasts and birthdays or if a special need is called for in the community. For most people, they can provide a simple introduction to ritual practices. The more advanced members of the community can use the occasion for socialization and to come in more direct contact with the Orisha through trance-possession.

SANTERÍA INITIATIONS

The first ritual usually undergone by those wishing to dedicate themselves to the Santería religion is Rogación, or Despojo. To outsiders, it would probably resemble a traditional baptism. The Rogación is performed to prepare an individual to enter the tradition. It is ceremonially designed to confer coolness, calm, clarity, refreshment, and rejuvenating power. It can be performed at several different locations ranging from a bathtub, to a baptismal font, to a stream. The process involves cleansing the head with a mixture of herbs, flowers, and spiritually imbued waters. The head is typically wrapped in white cloth and kept covered for an extended period of time ranging from one day, to a week, to even longer. Another unwrapping ritual takes place after the designated period of time. The ritual emphasizes the importance of the head in Santería or La Regla Lucumí. The head is the transition point for contact between the Orisha and humans. "Children," as the initiates are called, and all members of the community are thought of as having their head owned by a particular Orisha. By rejuvenating the head, the person is seen to have his or her whole being, including his or her connection to his or her patron Orisha, refreshed.

Typically, the next ceremony performed for the individual is the conferring of the Warriors. At this time, the practitioner is given the sacred tools and items of the Warriors (Elegguá, Ogún, and Ochosi). Again, the head is the focus of this ritual. A personal representation of Elegguá is conferred in the form of a small cement head with cowrie-shell eyes, although some ile still represent him more traditionally with a coconut. The cauldron of Ogún, along with his ceremonial iron tools, is also given at this time. As for Ochosi, a small iron crossbow called an *ache Ochosi* is used to represent his ashé in this context. Sometimes the necklaces (elekes, ilekes, or collares*)* will be given at this time. Each one represents the power of a specific Orisha, and they are worn in conjunction with each other to receive the protection of the energies. They are to be given specialized care and periodic feeding of animal offerings, and there are several taboos that must be observed while wearing them. Initiates are not allowed to wear them during sex or menstruation. The elekes are bathed in an *omiero*, or ritual liquid, to consecrate them initially. In certain parts of New York and Los Angeles, the necklaces have become a status symbol. Some gangs even use them as member identification.

The following is a very brief list of the types of elekes for some of the Orisha:

Eleggúa—Red and black beads

Ochosi—Green and brown beads, or blue and amber beads

Osanyin—Beads in his three colors (white, red, and yellow) as follows: One white bead is followed by nine red beads and then eight yellow beads, repeated to the desired length

Oko—Pink and blue beads

Oyá—Black and white beads, or red and brown beads with black and white stripes

Orunla—Yellow and green beads

Changó—Red and white beads

Obatalá—Twenty-one white beads followed by a coral bead

Oshún—Coral and amber beads, or gold and yellow beads

Yemaya—Crystal and blue beads

The Warriors initiation is the first full dedication a person takes to a particular spiritual house and family. From this point, the bulk of this person's spiritual knowledge is to be obtained from this family. Spiritual lineage is extremely important in Lucumí, as each member of the house is said to be a reflection of the beliefs, practices, and power of that congregation.

The crowning—and last, for many individuals—initiation in the tradition is the Asiento, also known as the Kariocha, to literally place the gods atop the head. A person may study for years, or even decades, for this initiation, which can only be given if the Orisha say so via divination. After this ceremony, the devotee is considered a Santero or Santera, *padrino* (godfather) or *madrina* (godmother), similar to a priest or priestess. From a sacred standpoint, it marks the death, rebirth, and empowerment of the initiate. It settles him or her as a child of a particular Orisha and, as such, he or she will be especially dedicated to that Orisha for the rest of his or her life. The process frequently involves extended ceremonies of seclusion, baths, dietary requirements and restrictions, and an extended period of dressing in white. Both in Cuba and the United States, the ceremony is an expensive one, ranging from $5,000 to $25,000 or more, depending on the spiritual house and the particular Orisha being received. This expense covers various offerings of food and drink, ceremonial tools, weapons, flowers, assistants, drummers, babalawo, and other components. As a financial hardship for the practitioner, this initiation symbolizes the burden of sacrifice required to attain such a great gift of power. One African-trained babalawo explained that the financial component is a New World adaptation. Originally, the devotee would pledge his or her services to the ile for a period of years. For the extended stay, the person would function as a live-in cleaner, handyperson, cook, gardener, and all-around assistant. In the current climate of the Western world, with both time considerations and the high value of money in this culture, most houses prefer to impose a financial responsibility on the situation instead. After the Asiento, the participant is given a new name and new white garments, is bathed by the other members of the house, and begins to become a representative of his or her particular Orisha. Some houses require their newly initiated to observe strict precautions, such as wearing white, maintaining abstinence, no cutting of the hair, and other requirements for a year or longer.

DIVINATION

Divination is of great importance in this religion. Almost nothing of significance is attempted without consulting either the shells with the Ifá divination tray (called the *diloggún*), or the coconut, also known as *obi*. The most basic of divinations in Lucumí are performed with a coconut. It is consulted frequently by devotees to answer simple yes-or-no questions. Any Orisha or ancestor may be contacted via this method. The diloggún is a form of divination with cowrie shells. Cowrie shells are a type of seashell from Africa that is used in groups of 16 to predict the future. *Throwing the shells* is another term for this most important form of divination in Lucumí. The rituals involve interpretation, questions, advice, and proverbs. The session helps to unify and organize a devotee's position in the physical and spiritual worlds. Divination always relates to the sacred destiny or path of the petitioner. The principle operating here is that there is a proper path or road for each individual to be on. The devotee's responsibility is to stay as close to that path as possible, so the need for repeated divinatory consultations is obviously apparent.

Often, divination reveals that a certain sacrifice is necessary to honor or appease the Orisha and, consequently, improve the troublesome situation at hand. The sacrifice can be understood as being imbued with the difficulties or blocks in the path, and literally handed over to the Orisha. For example, a reading for an initiate suffering problems with fertility could involve leaving an offering at the river for the Orisha Oshún to ask for her blessings and intercession.

PALO MONTE OR PALO MAYOMBE

The Palo Monte, or Palo Mayombe, traditions are often maligned as the darker sides of the Lucumí tradition. Like other African Diasporic Traditions, they focus heavily on trance-possession and mediumship. Also similar to some of the other traditions, they have practices that can lead toward both positive and negative manifestations of energy. The practices stem from the Congo religion of sub-Saharan Africa. Much of what takes place in the traditions is done under the cover of extreme secrecy, which could be part of the reason they often get misunderstood by Orisha worshippers. The traditions are to be kept separate, and yet many people actually practice both traditions, as they perform different-yet-important functions.

There is no strict hierarchy of divinity in Palo Mayombe, but the following are all honored in the tradition. Strong, powerful, and with no holds barred, Lucero occupies the space of the crossroads. The god of iron is Sarabanda. He is sometimes represented by images of Saint Peter or Saint Michael. One Palera (Palo priestess) I know has a protection chant that says, "Saint Michael above, Saint Michael below, Saint Michael, Saint Michael wherever I go." Siete Rayos is the divinity of seven flashes of lightning. Similar to Changó, he is petitioned to bring about speedy magickal results. Obatalá is linked to Tiembla Tierra, or Mama Kengue, in Palo. He is seen as the owner of the Earth and even the entire universe. Queen of the Water is known as Madre de Agua (mother of the waters) or Siete Sayas (seven skirts) in Palo Monte. She is a symbol of divine maternity revered by all. The river is also represented in Palo as the goddess Mami Chola. She is offered fresh river water and gold. The god of sickness and infectious disease is worshipped in Palo as Pata é Llaga or Tata Funde. Like Babaluaiye in La Regla Lucumí, he is seen as a miracle worker when it comes to healing. Centella Ndoqui is the warrior goddess of lightning and change. She is the mistress of the ancestor energy.

SANTERÍA CALENDAR

January 1—Feast for Elegguá, the trickster who resides in the crossroads

January 17—Feast for Osanyin, the masterful lord of herbalism

February 2—Festival for Oyá, the windy mistress of the dead

July 10—Alternate feast day for Aganyú

July 25—Feast for Aganyú, Orisha of the volcano

September 8—Feast for Yemaya, mother of the ocean

September 9 or 12—Feast for Oshún, Orisha of love and gold

September 24—Feast for Obatalá, king of the white cloth

September 27—Feast for Ibeji, the divine twins

October 4—Feast for Orunmilá, Orisha of divination

November 25—Feast for Obá, wife of Changó

December 4—Feast for Changó, lord of fire, drumming, and passion

December 17—Feast for Babaluaiye, Orisha of illness

PATAKIS
THE DIVINE LEGENDS OF SANTERÍA

Patakis are the divine legends of the Orisha. They correspond directly to divination outcomes. Every element in them reinforces both the religion of La Regla Lucumí and the individual who lives within the blessed boundaries of the religion. Not necessarily interpreted as literal stories, they teach lessons and warn of pitfalls on the path of existence. Some are based on stories from West Africa, and some are a fusion of indigenous Cuban and Puerto Rican mythologies. Patakis helped to transmit sacred lessons through their skillful retelling. Enslaved Africans were frequently forbidden to write, so the Patakis were one of the few ways they were able to transmit sacred knowledge. Each Orisha has many different Patakis to help situate him or her in the religious structure and to form a moral and social code.

Ochosi is the quintessential hunter, but as so often happens, his gift is his plight. The classic myth about Ochosi tells of a time when his village was suffering a great famine. All of the precious crops were ruined, and the hunters had not been able to catch any prey. Ochosi set out on a lifesaving hunt to catch food for the village. He was gone for several weeks before he was finally successful. When he returned home, he found that someone had killed and eaten his sacred pet bird. This bird had been his trusted magickal accomplice for many years. Understandably, Ochosi was incredibly furious. He shot one of his magickal arrows into the sky, aiming it for whomever had committed this sacrilege. It took flight and eventually came to rest in the heart of his beloved grandmother. Ochosi was besieged by guilt, a characteristic that still remains with him today. Even Ochosi's children, or devotees, are said to be prone to feeling guilty or regretful.

Obatalá wished to go and visit their son, Changó, who was ruler of the neighboring kingdom. Obatalá performed the necessary divinations and was told to delay the journey. However, their mind told them that the rains were about to start soon, which could ruin the journey altogether. Regardless, they ignored the warning of Ifá (god of divination) and set out on their journey. The first day went well, as Obatalá made great time and was very pleased with themselves. The next day they were awakened by a small black dog jumping on them. The dog was dirty, and Obatalá's robes, which were known for being the purest white, became stained. Obatalá considered going back home, but they decided it was "just a little dirt." They were still feeling good and they wanted to proceed. So, they did. After a few hours of traveling, Obatalá became hot. Seeing a refreshing stream, they decided to get a drink. The rocks by the water's edge were slippery, and they fell into the stream. They got soaking wet, and their pristine white clothes were now even more filthy. Since Obatalá was almost to Changó's palace, they decided to continue. When they arrived at the palace and stood at the gate, the guards began questioning, "Who are you? What do you want?" Obatalá replied, "I am Obatalá and I have come to see my son." The guards burst out laughing, for this was not the resplendent king of the white cloth they saw before them. Instead, they saw a dirty beggar and locked them away. Obatalá remained jailed for a year and a day until Changó accidently noticed them among the prisoners and released them immediately. This story is meant to reinforce the fact that everyone, even the king, must follow the guidelines of divination.

SANTERÍA BOTANICALS AND STONES

(*Note*: I recommend learning both common names and Spanish names for herbs and other common items.)

Basil (*Albahaca*)—All-purpose herb for all the Orisha

Chamomile *(Manzanillo)*—Love, joy, and prosperity

Changó thunderstone *(Piedra de Rayo)*—Use for calm during storms, for passion and courage

Coconut *(Obi)*—Success, purification

Cocoa butter—Sacred to Obatalá, use to bring on calm

Eucalyptus—Healing, money

Frangipani—Sweet scent used to attract love

Ginger *(Jengibre)*—Spiritual power

Lodestone *(Piedra de Iman)*—Use to attract good fortune

Moses in the Cradle *(Peregún)*—Transformation

Parsley *(Perejil)*—Healing

Pine *(Pino)*—Exorcism, money

Rosemary *(Romero)*—Use for cleansing to remove negativity

Rue *(Ruda)*—For exorcism, to ward off the evil eye

Spearmint *(Yerba Buena)*—Calm, tranquility, comfort, peace

Violet *(Violeta)*—Healing, peace, calm

PERSECUTION AND PROSECUTION

The United States' first occupation of Cuba occurred from 1898 to 1902. Ever since, there has been an uneasy relationship between the island and its neighbor. The Cuban Revolution took place in 1959, and persecution of the religion of Santería, or La Regla Lucumí, began only three years later and continued until the mid-1980s. Cuba, as a nation, was officially considered an atheist state until 1992. I have heard more recent stories, though, of a public statue of the Virgin of Caridad del Cobre, the patron saint of Cuba who also represents Oshún, being dressed in combat fatigues in a public square in Havana.

Things have not been easy for Santería practitioners outside of Cuba, either. The question of animal sacrifice and Santería made it all the way to the U.S. Supreme Court in *Church of Lukumí Babalu Aye v. City of Hialeah* (1993). The Church of Lukumí Babalu Aye has existed since 1973 and is run by Italero (priest) Ernesto Pichardo. Its mission was to bring the practices of Santería, including ritual sacrifice, out into the open. The church hoped to open a school, museum, and a cultural center. Problems arose when the city of Hialeah, Florida, passed an emergency ordinance designed to prohibit Santería's sacrificial practices.

The Florida laws had banned the animal sacrifices because they deemed them "unnecessary." Hunting for sport, euthanasia, and eradication of pests were all deemed necessary. The state in 1975 even upheld that citizens were allowed to use rabbits for the necessary practice of training greyhound dogs. The Supreme Court eventually decided that the ritual sacrifice of animals in connection with the religion of Santería is legal. Pichardo has gone on to publicize the religion and its practices.

Many of the ways of Lucumí have since come out of the shadows. The size of almost every ile I know has increased dramatically over the past 30 years. The Orisha seem pleased to expand their ashé respectfully and honorably throughout the Americas and the world.

CHAPTER FIVE
SHANGÓ AND OBEAH
CONNECTION AND CONJURE

SHANGÓ AND ORISHA
THE TRADITIONS OF TRINIDAD

The Orisha tradition has its own unique manifestation on the island of Trinidad. Here, the worship is often termed Shangó in honor of the lord of fire, drumming, and thunder.

The slaves who were originally brought to Trinidad were relatively diverse. They came from many tribes, including the Hausa, Igbo, Susu, Mandingo, Temne, Kissi, Fulbe, Kwakwa, and Congo. During the 1830s and 1840s, the ` grew in number and the religion became firmly established. The religion here, as in other areas, was discouraged and eventually prohibited by law with the Shouters Prohibition Ordinance of 1917, which disallowed all African-based ceremonies.

The spiritual pantheon here consists of some regulars such as Eshú, Ogun, Oshún, Yemanja, Shangó, Osain, and Oyá. There are also others that seem to be unique to the tradition: Mama Latay, Aireelay, Kufe, Gurum, Aba Lofa, and Palara.

There is also a strong legion of ancestor spirits sometimes referred to as Re-res. Modern practices also incorporate beliefs and practices from the different cultures that settled here, like Hinduism, Kabbalah, Spiritism, and other traditions. Here, there is a blurry line surrounding tradition. Several have observed a high concentration of different traditions, such as Kabbalah and Hinduism, mixed in with the African-derived forms of worship.

Ogun

Here, the first Orisha to arrive is usually Ogun. He behaves aggressively and often diagnoses illnesses of those in attendance at the ceremonies.

His colors are red and white. Ogun is given rice, corn, rum, and goat as offerings.

Osain and Aireelay

Osain is the lord of the jungle and the plants that live inside it. He is often represented by the image of Saint Francis. Osain is offered rice, black-eyed peas, and turtle.

The Orisha Aireelay, or Ajaja, is associated with Saint Jonah.

Shangó

Although the Orisha religion in Trinidad is often referred to as Shangó, the deity Shangó is also given the name Aba Koso. This probably stems from the Yoruba prayer or greeting of honor for the deity, Oba Koso, which has been said to roughly translate to "King of Koso." His colors are white and red. He is fed offerings of corn, rum, and rice.

Aba Lofa

Aba Lofa, or Elofa, is a rare deity who is not honored in many temples. He is rarely present at rituals, and when he is, he acts as an old man who moves slowly. His function is often to bless the children of the congregation. Aba Lofa is offered beef and rice.

Omira

The Orisha Omira is sacred to hunters and those who provide for the members of the community. He is often represented by the image of Saint Raphael.

Mama Latay

Mama Latay, or Omela, is an Earth Orisha. She is seen as maternal and nurturing. Her color is brown or brown plaid, and she is fed potatoes and root vegetables. The invocation for her usually follows Ogun.

More about the structure of Afro-Caribbean ritual can be found in a later chapter. There is currently a nominated Council of Elders in place in Trinidad that examines the religion and tries to publicize its practices.

This council is set up to alleviate some of the problems that occur when people have negative images and are prone to prejudice.

Ebejee

Unlike Santería, here the deity Ebejee is not evocative of twins but of Saint Peter as a fisherman. Ebejee is seen holding his keys and is often represented by the colors red and yellow.

Da Lua and Da Logee

The divine twins in this pantheon are called Da Lua and Da Logee. They are represented by images of Saint Jude (the patron saint of impossible causes) and Saint Simon (petitioned for divine justice), respectively.

Yemanja

Yemanja, Emanje, or Manja, is similar to the sea goddess of the same name present in other African Traditional Religions. She is a very powerful water goddess whose color is blue.

OBEAH TRADITIONS
IN BELIZE AND JAMAICA

Several Caribbean countries such as Jamaica and Belize feature a form of African-derived belief that is generally referred to as Obeah. Some say the origin of the word stems from the word for "snake," while some believe its etymology comes from the word for "witch." The tradition encompasses a variety of practices: herbal knowledge, honoring ancestors and other spirits, healing, divination, and protection. Obeah, like the Hoodoo practices of the southern United States, relies heavily on the use of independent practitioners crafting herbal preparations. In 1760, the religion was officially outlawed in Jamaica; this legal action was ostensibly responsible for inciting rebellion. The religion became increasingly associated with sorcery and unseemly magickal practices such as hexing. However, the tradition has continued throughout the years, and several practitioners keep using their spiritual knowledge to effect positive change. Oswan Chamani of the Voodoo Spiritual Temple was a great Obeah man from

Belize. After he passed over to the next life, he sent the following message to his wife and partner, Priestess Miriam:

> *Ah! ... The Heavenly gate open wide for me!*
> *I fasten well upon my seat.*
> *And if I should ride well upon the street,*
> *Of life Shall I seek.*
> *Oh! ... Ring the Bell.*
> *Hang on the steeple.*
> *At the Heavenly Gate I sleep.*
> *AH! ... My, what fate.*
> *Oh Gee ... I skated well*
> *Through the snake*
> *AH! ... The key to the estate?*
> *And finally*
> *I enter into the Heavenly Gate!*

Myalism

Myalism is the term given to the Obeah practices of Jamaica and Belize that involve rituals with dancing, drumming, and possession by the spirits. It comes from the term Myal Dance, which originated in West Africa. Over the years, its practices have become increasingly rare.

There is also a range of practices in Jamaica referred to as Kumina, or negatively as Pocomania. This religion is open to the interpretation of the spiritual elder. It involves a combination of African- and European-based practices.

Several of the Obeah spells are formulated to stop your enemies, sometimes "dead" in their tracks. Therefore, a lot of unusual physical items are used in the tradition, such as urine, menstrual blood, hair, sweat, teeth, and the like.

Duppies

Duppies are the frightening stuff of legend throughout Jamaica and the West Indies. They are the bogeymen, evil incarnate, that are conjured up and sent through the night to eat the naughty. A duppy is a dead soul set about to do the conjurer's bidding.

Bob Marley, the reggae legend, even sings about a duppy conqueror. Young Jamaican children are told the duppy will come for them if they don't eat their vegetables. This sensationalist folklore has, over the ages, become fused with tales about zombies.

Duppies and zombies both are people who have been drugged for one reason or another and are consequently slow-moving, dim-witted, and possibly mute. Zora Neale Hurston was the first academic to theorize that zombies were probably the result of some herbal potion. But it wasn't until almost 50 years later that Wade Davis, an ethnobotanist from Harvard, discovered the exact formula. It involves several unusual ingredients, including a poisonous fish.

SACRED ART OF TRINIDAD AND BELIZE

Trinidad, Belize, and several of the other Caribbean nations have their own manifestation of ancestor tribute. It is called the "bottle tree." Seen predominately throughout the Caribbean and the southern United States, bottle trees are living trees with multicolored glass bottles either covering or hanging from the ends of the branches. There is evidence that a similar practice dates back to Africa to approximately 1600 B.C.E. Each bottle is believed to symbolically represent a different ancestor spirit. Practitioners add to the tree frequently, either when someone has passed on or when a new ancestor spirit presents him- or herself during divination or a dream. These trees become living family legacies.

SHANGÓ AND OBEAH CALENDAR

June 29—Feast for Saint Peter, associated with Ebejee, the fisherpeople

September 20—Feast for Saint Raphael, associated with the Orisha Omira, the hunter

October 28—Feast for the divine twins, Da Lua and Da Logee, represented by Saint Jude and Saint Simon

December 4—Shangó Feast Day, for the lord of drumming and passion

JAMAICAN FOLKLORE

This is one of the most popular folklore stories from Jamaica. It tells of the trickster Anansi and his Brother (Brer') Dead.

Early one fine day Anansi was walking down the road when he saw Brother Dead sitting in front of a barbecue with a large stack of meat. Anansi walked over. The meat looked good to him and he said, "Hey, Brer', how's it going?" Brother Dead said nothing, so Anansi spoke again, "Brer', I a powerful hungry mungry. I take me piece?" Anansi grabbed a piece and walked off.

The next day Anansi went back and the same thing happened, but this time he told him he would bring back his daughter, Cindy, tomorrow to help Brother Dead with his work. So the next day Anansi and Cindy went to see Brother Dead. Anansi said, "Hey, Brer', I see you got you some meat. My daughter, Cindy, here to help clean, you no mind I take some meat?" Brother Dead said nothing, so Anansi said, "I gwine, I take some meat," and he left. The next morning he came back. Brother Dead was sitting there with a bow and arrow in his hand and Cindy had a ring on her finger. Anansi said, "I make you speak now Brer'." With that he took Brother Dead's long hair and tied half to one side of the barbecue, and half to the other side of the barbecue, and turned up the flame. But Brother Dead got free and followed Anansi all the way back home, where he was hiding in the loft with his wife and six children. They were up there for a long time, and the children got hungry, so Anansi came up with a plan. He told them to jump, and they did. One, two, three, ... Brother Dead caught them in his hands. By numbers 4, 5, and 6 Brother Dead's hands were getting full. Then Anansi and his wife both jumped down at once. Brother Dead dropped everyone in his hands to the ground, and that is why spiders like Anansi are found on the ground today.

OBEAH HERBS

At night, surrounded by the grandiose plants of the tropical forest, the Obeah men and women create herbal spells and charms for healing, protection, power, money, and anything else they can think of. The following is a partial list of ingredients they use:

Allspice—Protection, success

Cigar plant—To remove all obstacles in your way

Guava—Passion

Ginger—Joy and success

Hemp seed—Clarity and healing

Hibiscus—Also called "Jamaica flower," this is used for love and harmony

Lime—Cleansing; place in mouth so you will say the right thing

Lemon—Peace

Magic flower (*Achimenes* species)—For luck and success in all your magick

Sansevieria Snake Plant—Protection, power over evil

Pimento—Protection, negotiations

Nutmeg—For peace and love

Cinnamon—For invisibility

Bean sprouts—Love

Cloves—Love

White lilies—Psychic power, communication with the dead

Orchid—Love, luck, visions

FUTURES AND FIGHTING

I feel differently about the future of Shangó and Obeah, compared to that of the other African Traditional Religions. On the one hand, Shangó seems to be going strong. The Council of Elders and the number of spiritual houses can be seen as positive signs for the future of the religion. On the other hand, Obeah still seems to be trying to hold its own. Obeah had to first contend with oppression from the colonial masters, and then from the people practicing Myal, many of whom tried to discredit Obeah as being evil and focused on black magick. I even read an article the other day where the Christian churches in Jamaica were protesting that the Obeah practitioners were taking all the church money away by conning church members into buying spells and charms. They claimed that Obeah men made over $8 million a year from psychic readings. So the misconceptions continue, and the future of Obeah men and women, until they really start making $8 million a year, is uncertain. In the years since I have written these words, time has taken its toll on the Obeah religion, and there are fewer practitioners than ever.

CHAPTER SIX
AFRICAN TRADITIONAL RELIGION IN BRAZIL
A COMMUNITY, A SPACE, A DANCE, AND A RELIGION

CANDOMBLÉ

As in the case of several of the other religions described here, the people of Brazil put their own unique stamp on the Orixa traditions rooted in Yoruba cosmogony. Here, the language is Portuguese and the deities are called Orixa, and while they may have similarities to the Orisha in this book, they also feature their own unique differences. There are many different variations of the customs manifesting in the religions of Candomblé, Umbanda, Quimbanda, Spiritism, and others.

The earliest accounts of the word Candomblé date to 1826, or even possibly 1807, according to Rachel E. Harding. The word simultaneously refers to a religion, a community, a space, and a dance, all occurring mostly in Brazil. The first formations of the religion are believed to have started in Bahia, Brazil, long famed for its adherence to the ways of traditional Africa. As early as the 1830s, adherents there began a return to the African continent to replenish the spiritual knowledge. Candomblé utilizes words, music, and dance to honor the link to the ancestors across the ocean in Africa.

There is much historical evidence of African influence in the religions of Brazil. For example, one of the earliest records dates back to 1618. An informant named Sebastian Beretto reported to the Jesuit priests an African-derived funeral practice of slaughtering animals and using the blood as a sacrifice to ensure passage to heaven. The country also had its own version of witch trials. In 1744, Louisa Pinto was convicted of practicing the craft and presumably making a pact with the devil. Elsewhere, there are also positive descriptions of the colonial Portuguese praising the African enslaved people's phenomenal powers of healing. Because the Brazilian terrain was (and is) so vast, many times Europeans were in desperate need of whatever type of medical attention was available; even in the cities there was a shortage of physicians and apothecaries. African practitioners excelled as *curanderos,* or healers, for both fellow Africans and Europeans. In this way, part of the religious practices was allowed to remain out in the open.

The Brazilian experience with African religion is one that is characterized by duality. On the one hand, the Europeans were tolerant, even solicitous, of the Candomblé practitioners' knowledge and services. They frequented them for both medical and spiritual reasons, in the form of potions and spells. On the other hand, the Afro-Brazilian practitioners were frequently prosecuted for their actions. The initial criminal code of 1831, which was the first to deal with the subject specifically, prohibited acts that did not respect the state or uphold public morality. It is easy to understand how this loose wording could have been used to suppress the slaves' mass assemblies and religious sacrifices. By the 1870s, routine raids were occurring on the Brazilian "houses of fortune," or spiritual meeting houses, where all the participants were incarcerated.

The cruel institution of slavery was officially outlawed in Brazil in 1888, and up until that time a steady stream of slaves was sent to the country. With the increase in enslaved people, the practices of Candomblé multiplied. Within the religion they were able to retain some of the practices of their African heritage. The end of slavery, however, did not bring about the end of religious persecution of the imported Africans and Afro-Brazilians. Unfortunately, that was a long time coming.

More recently, the public face of Candomblé has finally come out of the shadows. In the 1990s, Varig Airlines launched an ad campaign urging its potential customers to "Fly with Axé" (similar to ashé). The ramifications of the public unveiling of the practices has yet to be fully realized.

The center of the Candomblé religion is called the *terrerio*, which is a structure for generating and containing axé. It stores the magickal items of the congregation and provides space for rituals. It is ruled traditionally by a priestess aided by a group of followers who worship the Orixa.

Exú: The Devil at the Crossroads

Exú is the lord of the crossroads, gates, doors, and open paths. Walking crooked and backward, he can be counted on to do the unexpected. He represents pure, unfocused energy and potential. Many of the negative impressions associated with the Exús and Pomba Giras (there are multiple manifestations of the divinity) come from their association with the devil and Jezebel, respectively. This follows from the descriptions sometimes given in Hoodoo traditions and some Latin American forms of African and folk religion of the man at the crossroads as the devil. This devil does not, however, embody evil as the Christian concept would like us to observe it. This devil, also described as *tio,* or "uncle," clears your roadways, removes your obstacles, and bestows talent in whatever form you request it, be it sexual prowess or even gold strikes. Obtaining these gifts requires devoted ritual on the part of the individuals by returning to the crossroads several nights in a row and waiting for Exú to appear. However, there is no evidence to suggest that these are *Twilight Zone*-like deals with the devil. On the contrary, accounts of meeting Exú have the feel of a pleasant exchange with an otherworldly passerby.

Pomba Gira: Sacred Sensuality

Pomba Gira dances at the crossroads of the sacred and the sensual. She is known as the consort/wife of Exú in Candomblé and other Afro-Brazilian religious traditions. She and her husband occupy a place "above and beyond" the other Orixa. They are the owners of the sacred crossroads and are the appointed messengers between the worlds of the visibles and invisibles. No ritual work is to begin without asking their permission.

There are many different faces of Pomba Gira: Pomba Gira Signa (the Gypsy), Gira-Mundo (World Spinner), Sete Encruzilhadas (Seven Crossroads), Pomba Gira das Almas (two souls), Pomba Gira das Cobras, Maria Padilla, and Maria Mulambo, to name just a few of the innumerable avatars who exist. Pomba Gira Signa specializes in problems with legal matters and justice. Sete Encruzilhadas throws her body backward when she manifests during possession. She is petitioned to assist with difficult or impossible problems, and her powers are enormous when she chooses to work her magick. This divine lady of the Seven Crossroads rules over destiny. Maria Padilla is one of the most well-known of all the Pomba Giras. She is believed to have been an actual Brazilian woman who has now become a deity that offers hope to women with relationship problems. Maria Mulambo is a no-nonsense woman dealing with punishment and jealousy. It is said she can solve any kind of problem.

Pomba Gira statues. – [photo by author]

Throughout history and cross-culturally, the place where two roads cross has been a site of divine inspiration and magick. Many different gods parallel the actions and attitudes of Pomba Gira and Exú. The Greek god Hermes was also a charming crossroads trickster deity. Like his Afro-Brazilian counterparts, he, too, was a messenger of the divine, with legendary sexual vigor and cunning. The darker reputation of Pomba Gira and Exú is shared with a different Greek deity, Hekate. She, too, was in charge of the crossroads of the night, and her association with the otherworldly often inspires fear and terror, just like Pomba Gira.

One of Pomba Gira's most notable qualities is that of open sensuality and freedom. This may also be a partial cause for her negative associations. She is often depicted in lewd and raunchy poses, frequently with her breasts bared. Her love of the corporeal pleasures and hedonism often find people comparing her with the goddess Oxum. Indeed, many of her sacred offerings are the same, including hoop earrings, necklaces, rings, and expensive perfumes. Like Oxum, she is in charge of matters of the heart. Pomba Gira's prowess is invaluable in removing obstacles blocking your path toward love and happiness. She undulates with joy and mirth. Pomba Gira is embodied by celestial twinkling laughter that emanates like a music from inside her.

She shares many of the same traits as Exú. For example, they both prefer the colors red and black or white and black. Her offerings, other than those mentioned, are black and red candles, cigarettes, hard cider, and roses (be sure to remove all thorns because she hates getting pricked without getting paid). One important factor in leaving offerings is that it is advised to place a small offering at the start of your dealings with Pomba Gira, and a larger, more elaborate offering (often called *pade* in relation to Exú) when she has granted you your desire. This, it is said, is because she prefers the larger payoff she gets at the end of your working. This multifaceted Orixa should be revered and remembered whenever dealing with Exú, especially in rituals relating to love.

Everyone interprets Pomba Gira slightly differently. Some see her as a beguiling force bringing the power to travel new roads and explore unknown possibilities. Her formidable power grants each of us a different lesson, a lesson we may not immediately understand but, hopefully, one we are able to enjoy.

Ogum: The Military General

Saint Anthony of Padua is the Catholic image most often linked with the Orixa Ogum. His possession dance is very military-like and often resembles a march. In ritual and in life, he provokes and protects.

Oxum: A Vision of Love

In Candomblé, Oxum, the Orixa of love, is seen as the wife of Ifá and, consequently, shares his powers of divination, which she may grant to women in her favor. She is also married to Oxossi. Oxum is fed grapes, eggs, and cakes.

Oxala and Ossain: Sky and Earth

Oxala is the sky creator of the Orixa. He is offered cool water and confers blessings of peace and rejuvenation.

Ossain, or Ossaim, is the Orixa of plants and herbs. He knows the secrets of curative herbalism.

Iemanja: Sea and Stars

Iemanja is the goddess whose name translates roughly to the mother whose children are the fish of the sea. In her avatar as Diosa del Mar, the Catholic image for the virgin rising from the ocean, she is considered the patron saint of Brazil. She is the mother of all the other Orixa. A goddess of the sea and stars, she can bestow great bounty.

Omolu: Sickness and Health

Omolu, Obaluae, or Sumbu, is the god of sickness, infectious disease, and healing. He has suffered, and with this sacrifice he has gained the knowledge of the power to heal. Believed by some to be the son of Nana Buluku, he uses his power of disease to punish as well as heal.

SPIRITISM

Spiritism is the name of the religion revealed by Allan Kardec. Kardec was a spirit who channeled himself through the body of French spiritist Hippolyte Léon Denizard Rivail. Rivail's mediumistic sessions with this spirit grew into the teachings of Kardecism. The defining tenets of this religion are a belief in the existence of spirits and reincarnation. Spirits are considered to be discarnated human beings who exist temporarily in the spiritual world. God is the supreme intelligence and primary cause of all things, including spirits who have been created to be first simple and ignorant, but with individuality and free will. Spiritual growth (seen as both intellectual and moral) requires reincarnating multiple times into the material world until achieving a maximum perfection where we are united with God. Interestingly enough, not all reincarnations are believed to take place on Earth, for there exist both inferior and superior worlds to this planet. Each incarnation is a chance to repair past mistakes and to speed up our spiritual evolution by helping humanity.

Kardec's revelations are thought to complement the teachings of Jesus, whose example is considered the ultimate model for human conduct. Of particular importance is Jesus' recommendation that we "love one another." Kardec, in imitation of Christ, proclaimed, "Without charity there is no salvation." Jesus' saying, "No one may see the Kingdom of Heaven if they are not born again," is cited as a proof of reincarnation.

Spiritists believe that it is possible for all levels of discarnated spirits (e.g., Pure Spirits, Good Spirits, Imperfect Spirits, to name a few levels) to communicate through a medium, but we are warned by Kardec to subject any information received to a rational analysis before accepting it as truth. A good medium is always one of high moral character rather than one of impressive special effects.

Spiritism declares that it respects all religions and applauds all efforts toward the practice of justice, love, and charity. Therefore, it is not surprising that, in one form or another, it has influenced many of the religions of the African Diaspora. The Brazilian Embassy lists over 1.5 million Spiritists in Brazil alone. To some extent, Spiritism has affected the religions of Umbanda, Quimbanda, and Macumba and even influenced the more established faiths of Candomblé and the Indigenous Brazilian religions. Some Spiritists have tried to discredit the practices of Umbanda and Candomblé, saying that the practices are too wild. In Cuba, Spiritism (Espiritismo) fused with elements of several other religions (i.e., Catholicism, Santería, Congo's Palo Monte, and Cuban aboriginal spirits) and evolved into Cuban Cordon Spiritism, or Espiritismo Cruzado.

⁕ UMBANDA AND QUIMBANDA ⁕

A purely Brazilian (therefore hybridized) religion, Umbanda's beginnings were solidified during the 1920s, and its practices still continue today. It is often difficult to separate this variant from other types of Brazilian religion. One of the reasons is that it does incorporate a variety of elements from African, Buddhist, Indigenous, and Hindu systems of thought. It has been consistently and continuously renegotiated over time by incorporating new Orixa.

Umbanda religious altar. – [Adobe Stock]

Umbanda *centros*, or ritual centers, proliferated throughout the 1930s. In 1941, the Primero Congresso de Espiritismo de Umbanda (First Congress of the Spiritism of Umbanda) took place in Rio. It set out to establish the parameters of the religion. Early on, a dichotomy was set up between Umbanda and Quimbanda as white and black, good and evil. A subsequent Afro-Brazilian response was mounted during the 1950s. Issues of class and race concerning the religion were brought to the fore. A clearer distinction came to be made between Umbanda Pura (a line deemed to be cleaner and purer) and the African-oriented forms of Umbanda. In the

Umbanda tradition, as in several other of those of the African Diaspora, practices are constantly shifting in Umbanda.

Umbanda possesses a group of honored individuals, not exactly full-fledged Orixa, but fed and consulted during ritual. They are called Pretos Velhos and Caboclos. They represent spirits of indigenous Brazilians and Afro-Brazilian slaves. Occupying an important legion of energies, they are given a privileged place. The Pretos Velhos, or honored slave spirits, are representative of the Africans' transformation after they were transplanted to the country of Brazil.

AFRO-BRAZILIAN MUSIC AND DANCE

Some Umbanda rituals do not feature drumming at all. Instead, ceremonies are accompanied by sacred songs and claps. The Orixa have their rhythms played on the very hands of the worshippers. Centros that do have drumming feature a typical set of three drums, as we have seen in the other African Diasporic Religions. Many of these are restricted by law as to where and when the drums can be played. Traditionally, the only places where drumming was allowed was in the *favelas,* or shantytowns on the city's edge. Still, the more African-influenced temples do retain drumming as a vital part of the tradition.

In Candomblé, participants dance clockwise or counterclockwise, depending on the occasion. Gradually, the moves increase in intensity. Learning the full battery of dances for the tradition can require months of study.

Much of the dancing done in both Candomblé and Umbanda ritual is for the Caboclos, the spirits of the Indigenous people of Brazil. There are two different types of Samba that can be employed for them: the Samba de Teste and the circle samba. The Samba de Teste is really a test given by the Orixa. This test could be dancing on hot coals or eating fire. It is done to prove the worthiness of devotees. They are not hurt performing these tasks but are instead given a special kind of spiritual protection and power. The circle samba is more of a formalized dance. Participants form an outside circle, and one or two people take turns dancing in the center to honor the Orixa. There are also ritual possession dances and movements in Umbanda. Ogum has a dance that is strong and forceful, pacing back and forth. The possessed makes sharp turns repeatedly while dancing with swords. Occasionally, mock swordfights and confrontations are staged by devotees. In many ways, this mimics the combative movements of the traditional Yanvalou dance of New Orleans Voodoo, and both were most likely used as coded symbols for slave revolt.

A MYTH OF BRAZIL

The lord Oxossi in the Candomblé pantheon is a supreme hunter. It is said that one day Oxossi went out into the forest and came across the divine serpent Oxumare. He captured him and brought him home for his wife, Oxum, to cook. When she pulled the snake from Oxossi's hunting bag, the snake began to sing. Oxum was shocked, having never heard such a thing. She refused to go near it again. So it was Oxossi who chopped up, cooked, and ate Oxumare, who was singing all the while. In Oxossi's stomach, the snake put itself back together and escaped. Oxossi ran after Oxumare, shooting and cursing. The serpent finally escaped to the castle of the king. There, Oxumare told his story, and the king remarked that Oxossi had become quite the "hunter." This distinction has continued ever since.

CALENDAR OF BRAZIL

September 27—Feast for the Ibeji, the sacred twins

January 1—Feast for Iemanja, the Orixa of the sea

Second Thursday in January—Washing of the Church of Bonfim Ceremony in Bahia, Brazil; this festival consists of a procession to the church and a ritual washing of the steps

BOTANICALS OF BRAZIL

The following list contains herbs used in either Candomblé, Umbanda, or Quimbanda. If you can, try to obtain fresh herbs, as they are believed to have the most axé.

Anise *(Anis)*—Used for protection and dreaming

Banana—For the dead

Bitter kola *(Orobo)*—Luck

Cashews—For the dead

Dracena fragrans *(Peregun)*—For the warrior Orixa: Exú, Ogum, and Oxossi

Mint—Wisdom and power

Palm oil *(Dende oil)*—Used to honor each of the Orixa

Papaya *(Momao)*—Healing

Rue *(Arruda)*—Protection

Sensitive plant *(Mimosa)*—For spiritual power

Wormwood *(Artemesia)*—Exorcism

A RELIGION COMES TO LIFE

In many ways, the African-derived practices of Brazil have been allowed to grow and expand more freely than in some of the other locations I have been discussing. I don't attribute this to any better treatment of worshippers, but instead to a geography that allowed them to escape and hide from their oppressors. Consequently, the practices have become intrinsically bonded with the culture of the Afro-Brazilians. One only has to look at films like *City of God* and *Dona Flor and Her Two Husbands* to see that Candomblé is a normal part of almost every aspect of life. Hundreds of thousands of people show up at the beach in Rio on New Year's Eve to get ready to praise and honor Iemanja, and every year that number continues to grow.

Worshippers clapping at the Festival of Yemanja in Salvador, Bahia, Brazil. – [Adobe stock]

CHAPTER SEVEN
SHRINES OF AFRICA AND BEYOND

Shrines and altars are a vital part of the religions of Ifá, Vodou, New Orleans Voodoo, Santería, Candomblé, Umbanda, Shangó, and Obeah. A shrine is set up inside or outside as a permanent tribute for the Lwa or Orisha. An altar can be described as a temporary creation designed to bring about a specific magickal result. The shrines and altars used in these traditions can be as simple as a glass of water or as elaborate as an entire dedicated room decorated with finery.

ALTARS AND SHRINES

The amount of time spent attending to religious prayers, offerings, and rituals for the average Voodoo, Santería, or Candomblé practitioner is extensive. Individuals often have daily prayers and offerings they must leave, in addition to weekly tributes and periodic obligations to the ile or hounfor. Frequently, practitioners have shrines that are set up as permanent areas for devotional worship in their homes. These must be cleaned and maintained regularly.

One comment I hear from many outsiders is their surprise at the sheer number of shrines in place in a Voodoo or Santería temple. At one time in my own home, I had over 26 distinct shrines to various deities. Items placed in these sacred spaces belong to the Lwa and Orisha and are not used or handled except for cleaning or ritual purposes. If you are a visitor to a temple's or practitioner's shrine area, please do not handle items or place your drink there, since doing so would be disrespectful. It is usually all right for visitors to leave offerings such as money, but if you are unsure, please ask first.

The same rule about respecting altar spaces also applies to those set up for a ritual. During a ritual, altars will usually be set up throughout the sacred space. Different Lwa or Orisha need their respective spaces during a ritual, and setting up multiple areas of worship addresses this problem. Again, it is usually OK to leave offerings, but check with one of the ritual assistants (called *hounsi* in Haitian Vodou, or *oriate* in Lucumí).

Shrines of the Ifá Faith

The Ifá faith originated with the Yoruba people throughout West Africa. Many were Nigerian, and the shrines created for the Orïsa there were located outdoors. Often, they included sacred trees, rocks, or other natural elements. The traditional Yoruba also worship at special areas in nature—for example, at a particular bend in the river. Several of the ancient Yoruba shrines were restored by Obatalá priestess Susanne Wenger and local artists Adebisi Akanji and Buraimoh Gbadamosi, along with others. During the 1960s and 1970s, these refurbishments took Orïsa art to a whole new level. Nontraditional elements were used like the curving cement wall outside the entrance to the Osun shrine in Oshogbo. Over the years, these have met with some controversy.

A shrine is simultaneously a site of beauty, honor, prayer, dedication, and belief. Traditionally, the Yoruba shrines of West Africa are in direct contact with nature. Often, there are communal shrine areas in the center of a town, open to the air. Many of their altars are also placed outside at the threshold or crossroads. For specific Ifá offerings, see chapter 2.

Sacred Shrines of Vodou

Eclectic, innovative, colorful, and extensive are all words that describe the shrine creations of the Vodou world. A shrine is just as likely to contain elements of the divine and the mundane. Cola bottles, perfume, feathers, and rocks are all normal items. In fact, the museum exhibit created by Donald J. Cosentino and documented in his book *The Sacred Arts of Haitian Vodou* even included a phallic cane covered with a condom. Vodou shrines are some of the most striking in the world. Detailed artistic portraits of Catholic saints hang beside tables of half-empty bottles and petrified frogs. The nontraditional artist Pierrot Barra even incorporates used baby doll heads from the garbage repository in Port-au-Prince's Iron Market.

The shrines here are frequently called *Pé* and can be laid out on the floor or on a table. They usually contain a Catholic saint statue or lithograph, along with vévés either on a flag or painted directly on the wall. As in Barra's art, dolls dressed in the appropriate colors for the Lwa are used. Most shrines also have a considerable number of bottles. These can be bottles of rum, tequila, wine, beer, Florida Water, and cola, as well as bottles that are designed to hold and fortify the spiritual energy of the members of the hounfor.

Maman Brigitte feast table. – [photo by Christian Bazan]

Compared to Lucumí, the shrines of Haitian Vodou are, in many ways, less decorative and more immediately functional as repositories for the souls of the congregation. They are also very utilitarian, containing all the offerings that may be needed by the houngan or mambo during a ceremony or consultation.

Voodoo Shrines of New Orleans

Due to the concentration of rituals surrounding the dead, many of the ceremonial art and shrine creations in New Orleans revolve around the honored ancestors. Several grave markers are fantastic homemade creations. They use techniques of mosaic and collage to incorporate just about anything onto the grave marker.

One unique feature of the area is the attention given to the altars of Marie Laveau. A few different statuary images of her are imported to the area from Bahia, Brazil. These representations are frequently found on the shrines of New Orleans, alongside pictures or miniature representations of her famous tomb and vévés as a tribute to her, either in flag form or painted on the floor. As I have mentioned, the continued worship of serpents has occurred here for over 150 years; consequently, altars sometimes incorporate cages or tanks for these blessed creatures.

Marie Laveau and Spirits of New Orleans. – [photo by Christian Bazan]

Ancestor altars are given a special place and prominence in the tradition. Many temples feature a shrine for the remembered temple dead as well as for Oyá, the Baron, and Maman Brigitte.

The Shrines of Santería

Santería, more properly known as Lucumí, contains some of the most elaborate shrine creations in the world. Decorated ornately, they are even referred to as *tronas* (thrones) of the Orisha. I have seen shrines that incorporate dozens of yards of expensive fabric and statues that stand over 6 feet tall. I have even seen a few spiritual houses that have fountains included in the design.

Shrines can be created in the ile or in a worshipper's own home. They can be permanent installations or set up temporarily for a specific feast or ceremony. In most households, however, they are typically set up in a separate room or a least a custom-made cabinet. Several yards of fabric are draped, gathered, and hung from the ceiling. Devotees can never really have too much fabric, and almost every Santera I know is constantly on the lookout for more. It can be used under, around, or over a shrine for the Orisha.

Color is very important and must correspond to the specific Orisha. There is, however, one exception that is unique to Santería. People may use the color of the Orisha who is married to the primary Orisha they are creating the shrine for. For example, a small amount of red could be used to honor Changó on an otherwise-all-yellow shrine for Oshún, his wife. Cleanliness is also important when setting up these shrines—everything must be absolutely clean. This represents the purity of intent and respect devotees have for the Orisha.

Lucumí shrines operate visually on many different levels. The ground or the floor is covered with a cloth on which food and candles can also be placed. Then a table or pillars are also covered with fabric, where statuary and other items of prominence are placed. Drums (*batá*) and sacred stones (*otanes*) can also be placed here. Finally, hanging from the ceiling is more fabric, typically silk and lace, plus candle holders, incense burners, and sometimes even balloons.

Shrines in Trinidad

One unique feature of the ceremonial constructs of Trinidad relating to the religion is the use of temple flags. In Haitian Vodou, as I have mentioned, flags are used like banners to be waved throughout the rituals, while in Trinidad the flags are permanent installations placed either outside or inside the temple compound. The flags are in colors specific to the Orisha worshipped at that temple and can serve as a marker for worshippers to help identify the space's spiritual affiliations.

Brazil: Shrines in the Land of the Living Statues

Bahia, Brazil, is the land of the statues. Several businesses in the area are set up to make Orixa statues for domestic and international use. Priest and author Jorge Amado even wrote a best-selling book called *War of the Saints* about an Orixa statue that comes to life. Here, these creations are treated as living representations of the Orixa. They eat, drink, and have even been known to move slightly.

Leaves infused with sacred water wait on a table for use in candomble axé blessings in the tourist center of Bahia, Brazil. – [Adobe stock]

One unique feature in Brazil is the use of statues for Exú. Unlike other ATRs—where Eleggúa/Eshú can be represented by a coconut or cement head—Exú here is given the image of the devil. Most of the shrines for the Exús (there are multiple manifestations of the divinity) are located in Rio de Janeiro, and they figure prominently in Umbanda and Quimbanda. Exú's wife, Pomba Gira, is also heavily favored there. The street corners are often the site for small altar offerings for Pomba Gira and Exú. The offerings can consist of red roses, beer, cigarettes, lit candles, and money. If someone wished to work with Pomba Gira, he or she would go to the crossroads at midnight where three roads meet, also called a T-stop. He or she would light the candle, leave the roses, ask for assistance with a problem, take three puffs from the cigarette, and leave it next to the candle with the money. The final step would be to promise Pomba Gira additional offerings once she offers her help. Then the person turns around and walks away without looking back.

The practices of Umbanda and Candomblé *terrerios* (temples) have different levels of African-influenced rites The less African-influenced of the Umbanda terrerios feature simple creations with possibly only a glass of water on a white table, while the more African-influenced shrines of Brazil are multileveled and complex, like those in Lucumí. They contain the *assentamentos* (seats) for the Orixa. Each assentamento is made up of an enamel or earthenware basin that holds the sacred items. These can include the otanes, *ferramentos* (iron tools for the Orixa), skulls, jewelry, pitchers of water, or herbal preparations. Each assentamento is for the ruling Orixa of a particular member of the terrerio. In conjunction with the assentamentos, the shrine can include flowers, vases, ribbons, candles, lights, and statues. On Umbanda altars, it is not unusual to see Catholic, indigenous, and African representations occurring simultaneously. Occasionally, the hierarchical structure of the religion is represented by giving the Orixa the highest position and placing the Pretos Velhos (honored spirits of enslaved Africans) and twins lower down.

Spiritist altars often include simply a glass of water to absorb negative energy, while Candomblé altars are elaborate and referred to as *peji*. They contain offerings from places as diverse as a Catholic church and the supermarket. Exú is honored with his traditional colors of red, black, and white. Often, his altar features a trident. Ogum, as in other traditions, is in charge of the ritual implements for sacrifice. Therefore, ritual knives and swords are placed on his altar. The Catholic images used to represent him are Saint Anthony and Saint George. Altars and shrines for Oxossi frequently emphasize his connection to the indigenous spirits and thus are frequently shown using headdresses, feathers, bows and arrows, and a spear. Iansa is the mistress of stormy lightning and the dead. Her altar represents her great power and magick. It often contains a sword, items of copper or brass, and antlers or horns. Ossain, the Orixa of medicinal and magickal plants, is frequently honored with wild-collected herbs. Altar items for Iemanja include vases and jars of seawater, roses, nail polish, and images of the ocean. Oxum is covered in gold, as in other African Diasporic traditions. The Ibeji also have a traditional form of representation: dolls, as in Haitian Vodou; toys, as in Lucumí, and various flowers, herbs, and candies.

The rainbow serpent is represented in Candomblé by the androgynous goddess Oxumare. The altar for this Orixa is in the ceremonial colors of yellow and green and is covered with offerings of cowries, corn, beans, and shrimp sautéed in dende oil. Xango, the Orixa of fire, is represented on the altars of Candomblé with thunderstones, a symbol that also occurs in Nigeria and Cuba. Drums and Xango's ritual mortar are also common elements.

Create an Ancestor Shrine

Not every practitioner called to serve is required to set up a shrine, but, under proper guidance, those who do are able to gain the favor of the Orisha in a different way than those who do not. Making a shrine is a spiritual exercise that teaches patience and aesthetic expression. Beginners of any and all traditions can start out by making an ancestor shrine.

In the various chapters in this book, I have repeatedly mentioned the importance of the ancestors or the dead in each of these African Traditional Religions. A good beginning way to initiate and strengthen contact with those who have passed is to set up an ancestor shrine. It should be located in a place of prominence in your home where you will see it frequently throughout the day. This is the time to let your creative energy and psychic intuition flow. Start with the remembered dead, relatives, close friends, and mentors who have passed. Do not include any pictures of the living. Eventually, we will all have a chance to be honored in this way when it is time. No need to rush. If you have photographs, artwork, jewelry, or anything else that belongs to these people, here is the perfect place for it. Certain practitioners like to place holy water, graveyard dirt, candles, flowers (real or silk), and food offerings here. Once the devotional space is set up, you can begin to have regular contact with it. A good way to do this is to leave daily offerings of coffee, alcohol, or something else your ancestors liked, along with your prayers. Some Babalawos I know even leave a portion of every meal on the earth for the ancestors. This continued contact should provide you with increased guidance from your ancestors.

St. Roch Cemetery No. 1, New Orleans. – [photo by author]

A Note for the Adopted

I am often asked by students how they can adapt this ritual if they have been adopted and are not familiar with their actual ancestral lineage. Not to worry—everyone can have a wonderful and productive ancestor shrine. Everyone on this Earth has gaps in their knowledge of their family tree, and the process of setting up this type of shrine always involves a lot of intuition and guesswork. Those without names and places to include should work with scrying and intuition. What names, locations, cuisines, and cultures are you drawn to? You should use these things as guidelines and expand from there.

CHAPTER EIGHT

VOODOO AND LUCUMÍ MAGICKAL WORKINGS

The subject of magickal workings in African Traditional Religion is a difficult one to describe adequately. In Lucumí and Vodou, spells and workings function in varying ways and intensities, depending on the level of proficiency. The Hoodoo practices of the southern United States are largely based on personal magickal spells to effect change, while in Lucumí almost all workings are performed in consort with others. In each one of these traditions, spiritual strength and power are built up over time through devotional offerings, rituals, and initiations. Consequently, there are only some types of spells that are suitable for people without initiation. Most of these relate to spiritual calm, cleanliness, and guidance. In all circumstances, I recommend divination and consultation with your spiritual teachers.

RITUAL CLEANSING AND BATHS

African Traditional religions have a strong focus on spiritual and physical calm and cleanliness. In Ifá, the Yoruba-derived religion from Nigeria, offerings of water are frequently left to provide the individual with rest and calm. A wonderful spell for bringing peace and clarity to yourself is to simply sit for one hour in silence with a glass of water and a lit white candle. This could also be performed in conjunction with a cleansing bath.

In La Regla Lucumí, magickal baths are taken for every purpose, from removing obstacles to success in life.

Cleansing Bath

This bath will remove confusion and bring calm to an individual. Take 3 cups spring water and place in a glass pot or bowl, then heat water to boiling. Add ¼ cup of fresh or dried basil. Remove it from heat and let it steep for 21 minutes before straining the mixture. Add 8 drops of lavender oil and 3 dashes of Florida Water (Florida Water is a common formula and is available online and even at some supermarkets). Store this mixture in a glass jar. Use healthy amounts in your bath during the waxing moon. This is a great preparation to make ahead and have on hand just in case things get stressful or confusing.

Crossroads Bath to Create Opportunities

Take 3 ounces of coconut water and add 3 drops of basil oil and 1 tsp. of vanilla extract. Mix with 1 gallon of spring water. Use as needed.

Psychic Power Bath

Use this bath to strengthen your psychic power. For best results, use every new moon. Mix ¼ ounce of parsley leaves, along with 1 drop of sandalwood oil and ¼ ounce of sage in 8 ounces of boiling water. Let it steep for one hour before straining through a cotton cloth. Add ¼ cup of the mixture to your bathwater.

Love Bath

Mix 1 cup river water, 5 drops orange oil, 5 drops rose water, 5 drops cinnamon oil, and 5 drops jasmine oil, then add 1 gallon spring water. Use 5 drops in your bath whenever you want to bring love into your life.

TO REMOVE UNWANTED INFLUENCES

Much of the practices of the Hoodoo, or southern folk magick tradition, grew out of the everyday necessity of solitary practitioners. Individuals needed quick and effective ways of dealing with their problems as they arose. This is why the practices consist of an extensive use of herbs and charms that can be used in a multitude of ways. In an earlier chapter, I mention the Hi John the Conqueror root and a few spells using that herb. The practices also use everyday items in a magickal way.

•» For Unwanted Houseguests

One of my favorite spells is to get rid of an unwanted houseguest. Take your common household broom and stand it, bristles upright, behind the front door. Then stab an ordinary dinner fork through the bristles while you imagine that person leaving. Leave the broom in place, undisturbed, until your mission is accomplished. You can then return the items to their usual place.

•» To Leave Your Troubles Behind

This Hoodoo spell to leave your troubles behind involves pennies. Hold three pennies (make sure at least one is marked with the current year), take a deep breath and exhale, blowing your troubles into the pennies. Then travel to a crossroads and throw the pennies behind you. Don't look back. Repeat this as needed.

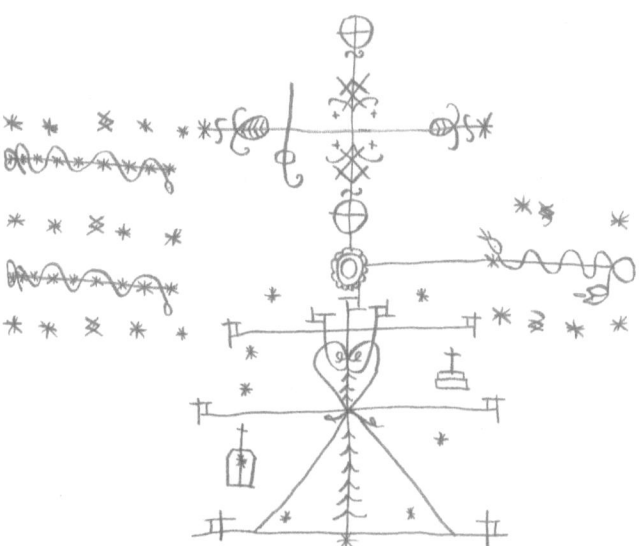

Milocan protection vévés which includes Papa Legba, Maman Brigitte, Damballa and Aida Wedo vévés.– [image by Tehron Gillis]

•» VÉVÉ MAGICK «•

New Orleans Voodoo and Haitian Vodou spells are almost always performed with the assistance of a mambo or houngan, in direct response to some difficulty or to honor the Lwa. The spells are designed to strengthen an individual's connection to one or more Lwa. In these traditions, véves are often used to contact and honor the Lwa. These can be drawn on parchment or other magickal paper and carried like a talisman. For example, if someone wanted to attract more love in his or her life, he or she might place the Erzulie véve written in Dove's Blood Ink (available at most psychic supply shops) in his or her pocket. Similarly, if someone had a concern when dealing with the medical profession, he or she could carry the véve for Ogou B'alindho (lord of medicine and surgery). Again, these are only rough guidelines, and a mambo or houngan must be consulted for all serious problems. These spells are in many ways like life: The more time, effort, and attention you devote to your desires, the more successful you will be.

RITUAL FEASTS

Feast days provide another opportunity for magick in African Traditional Religions. One of the largest feasts is that of Saint John, held on June 24. In the Catholic faith, he was responsible for cleansing and blessing the congregation. For hundreds of years, the celebration has included cleansings, feasts, and acts of charity. The day, which includes festivities beginning the night before, was said to be a favorite holiday for Marie Laveau, the Voodoo Queen. The next Saint John's Day, consider performing the following ritual to bring about much-needed blessings in your life. Donate 10 or more items to your local food pantry or food bank. At home, prepare your own feast for your friends and family, including, but not limited to, roasted meat or other protein, sweet potatoes, corn, and pastries. As you cook and eat, consider the connection between physical sustenance and spiritual sustenance. Know that by feeding yourself and others on this day, you have also fed your soul in many ways.

January 1 is also a major feast day. It is celebrated in Brazil as a major festival for Iemanje. Among Hoodoo practitioners, it is occasion for a ritual feast that must include collard greens for financial success and black-eyed peas for luck in the coming year.

Candle Spells

One of the spells I repeatedly give out to beginning students is a magickal working for the Orisha Ochosi. Ochosi is the celestial hunter and tracker in Lucumí, and in this spell he is given offerings in exchange for assistance in finding a spiritual teacher. To find the proper spiritual teacher, humbly ask Ochosi for guidance as you offer the following items: seven cigars, a pheasant feather, a mango, a glass of anisette, a good-sized piece of turquoise, and rosemary (*romero*). Gather all the items together along with a green or purple seven-day candle (the tall pillar candles in a glass container). Light the candle on the next new moon and concentrate on your request as you hold each item for a minute. Extinguish the candle with your fingers or by smothering it, and place it along with the other items in a safe place. On the eve of the full moon, place all the items on the open earth under a large tree. By the next full moon, you should begin to have new opportunities for study and spiritual growth, provided you keep looking for them.

Several of the spells used in New Orleans Voodoo and the other African Diasporic Religions involve the use of candles. Both novice and adept alike can use candles to strengthen and reinforce their magickal workings. White seven-day candles are the best all-purpose candle. They are suitable for just about every occasion. Often, practitioners add herbs, oils, and even glitter to candles to personalize them for their specific magickal needs. Please never leave a burning candle unattended.

Eleggúa Road Opener Candle

Use this candle when you feel like your road to success is blocked. Take a red seven-day candle and add to it a pinch each of pipe tobacco and coffee and a tiny drop of coconut oil. Light the candle every morning and concentrate on moving toward and achieving your goals. If you need to extinguish the candle, please do so by smothering it. This is said to preserve the power of the candle. Continue this until you feel like you have been successful.

·» Yemaya Candle

Use this candle to honor the Orisha of the sea. Place a blue candle in a bowl of water to which a pinch of sea salt has been added. To the top of the candle add a pinch of seaweed, rosemary, basil, and spearmint, 3 drops of lavender oil, and 7 drops of lemon oil. Light whenever you need peace and comfort. If, at any time when using candles in your spell, the candle puts itself out, begins to turn the glass a serious black, or the entire top of the candle is on fire, another type of spell is needed. There could be negativity or obstacles in your environment that need to be dealt with first. Please do not leave candles unattended.

Yemaya Candle spell to honor the Orisha of the sea. – [photo by author]

·» Computer and Electronic Help Candle

Take a green seven-day candle, add a small pinch each of black salt, black glitter, Abre Camino herb, and iron filings. Light the candle for seven minutes each day, beginning on a Monday, and concentrate on your desire, continuing until you have succeeded. When finished, bring the unused portion of the candle to a railroad track and leave it there along with seven pennies.

VOODOO DOLLS

Voodoo dolls are the stuff of B-grade horror movies and legend. In actuality, dolls that have pins stuck in them are rarely, if ever, used in Haitian Vodou. Some spiritual houses or temples use what can be called a little soul doll. These dolls are used as a sort of substitute body for an ancestor spirit. In this form the ancestors can be fed, cared for, and honored. Among the Zulu of South Africa, dolls are often used in healing magick, with the doll serving as a substitute for the sick individual. In New Orleans, Voodoo dolls are sometimes sold as guardian dolls for protection or as "mojo" dolls stuffed with Spanish moss and adorned with various charms and herbs designed to bring about a specific effect, such as luck. Again, it must be stressed that these are not created to bring harm to an individual and are only used for healing and protection.

GRIS-GRIS
A LITTLE BIT OF MAGIC

Gris-gris bags are magickal herbal bundles worn about the neck or other part of the body. Most likely, the earliest written record of these pertains to the gris-gris court case in 1773. They are popular in the New Orleans Voodoo and Hoodoo traditions. The following recipes can be prepared by mixing with a mortar and pestle and then placing in a small flannel or silk bag and worn until the desired result is achieved. To dispose of the bag, bury it under the largest tree you can find.

For traveling—Comfrey, thyme, and basil

For protection—Basil, black salt, sesame seed, sandalwood oil, and one cowrie shell

For love—Cinnamon, red rose petals, patchouli, rose quartz, and a seashell

For marriage (wear to bed to see visions of your new spouse)—Clove, allspice, baby's breath, hemp seed, and a gold coin

For lusty encounters—Musk, patchouli, and clove

To converse with the dead—Graveyard dust (graveyard dirt), cedar oil, dried blueberries, orange peel, wintergreen, eucalyptus, sesame seed, copal, and basil

For divine justice—Coconut, basil, raw cotton, and lime peel

For health—Bay rum, lavender, popcorn, basil, and witch hazel

For luck with playing cards—Dried apple, patchouli oil, and pine needles

For success—Juniper berry, patchouli, and peonia (aka huayruro or guairuro seed)

For dreaming—Lemon oil, rose petals, and sea salt

MAGICKAL OILS

Worshippers of African Diasporic Religions from Boston to Bahia, Brazil, all use magickal oils. Oils can be worn, added to a bath, sprinkled throughout the home, placed into a bowl of water under the bed, or added to lotion and rubbed on hands and feet. Wearing an oil allows your body to come into direct contact with its magickal energy throughout the day. And your home can be protected or magickally energized by placing a few drops of oil in the corners of each room. By adding magickal oil to a bowl underneath your bed, you will be able to affect your dreams. If you are having a problem with nightmares, try placing a few drops of Protection oil in a bowl of salt water underneath your bed. Oil, when added to a simple body lotion, can be applied to hands and feet to influence whatever you touch and wherever you walk. Small amounts of oils can also be dripped into candle wax and used that way to keep the energy burning.

If at all possible, carry out these works in secret; helpers are fine, but avoid anyone who may not be sympathetic to your mission. The very act of skeptical outsiders observing your magick will alter its effectiveness.

The following oil spells are based on traditional ATR formulas. One cup of sweet almond oil or olive oil can be used as a base for all these preparations. There is one quick cautionary note: Please choose your magickal intent wisely. These spells are general in nature so as to bring about the best possible result. Specific Voodoo and Lucumí spells, for example, to make a specific person love you forever, are possible but not recommended. In these situations, invariably what happens is the person achieves the desired result, but (at the very least) discovers it wasn't what was wanted or needed. Magickal intent and focus are very important, so try to concentrate on bringing the best possible situation to you.

•» Obeah Oil

For spiritual power.
3 drops vetivert oil, 9 drops galangal oil, 3 drops lemon oil, and 1 shark tooth

•» Animal Magnetism

This oil is designed to make you more attractive to both man and beast.
3 drops lilac oil, 3 drops cypress oil, and 3 drops lavender oil

•» Protection Oil

For protection against harm.
1 drop myrrh oil, 3 drops sandalwood oil, and 6 drops lavender oil

•» Spiritual Cleansing Oil

Use during the waning moon, the time for banishing evil.
7 drops sandalwood oil, 3 drops coconut oil, 3 drops vetivert oil, and 7 drops lime oil

⋙ Happiness and Success Oil

Wear to brighten your outlook and improve your chances for success.
3 drops heliotrope oil, 5 drops amber oil, and 5 drops rose oil

⋙ Oil for Divination

Use a small amount of this oil before divination. Caution: It may stain.
9 drops red palm oil, 9 drops lavender oil, and 9 drops bergamot oil

⋙ King Solomon Oil

This is a traditional Voodoo blend for wisdom and getting your own way; Solomon is revered in Voodoo because he knew the secrets of symbols, angels, and also demons.
3 drops sandalwood oil, 3 drops lemon oil, and 3 drops nutmeg oil

⋙ Get a Job Oil

Wear this oil when going on job interviews to make the best impression and to remove obstacles to your success. If you have a chance to do so undetected, sprinkle the oil around where the interview will take place.
3 drops basil oil, 7 drops peppermint oil, and 7 drops lilac oil

⋙ Healing Oil

Wear this oil or anoint a small piece of rose quartz and carry it with you at all times to promote health and healing.
10 drops vanilla oil, 3 drops rose oil, and 4 drops magnolia oil

⋙ Rose of Jericho Oil

This is an oil prepared as an infusion. Take a large glass jar and place the Rose of Jericho inside. Pour oil into the jar and close the lid. Leave the jar outside overnight, where it will catch the light of the full moon. In the morning, pour off the oil and use as needed to rejuvenate your finances.
Half-cup olive oil and 1 Rose of Jericho

•» Money Oil

Mix this combination in an oil base and add gold glitter and one tonka bean. Use this formula to anoint your money or wallet and use on candles around your place of business.

3 drops galangal oil, 3 drops lemon verbena oil, 3 drops nutmeg oil, 3 drops clove oil, gold glitter, and 1 tonka bean

These oil formulas may be used alone or in combination to achieve your desired results. They will increase in magickal potency over time and should be stored away from direct sunlight. One good idea is to trade magickal formulas with your friends, as their magickal strengths may be different from yours. I have more than one friend who I frequently trade formulas with so we can all increase the potency of our workings.

DIVINATION

There is no substitute for proper divination and consultation with your priest or priestess. Most people wouldn't try to fix their car if they weren't a mechanic. The priest and priestess are highly trained professionals who are able to find out what is really the cause of your problems and advise or even carry out the necessary actions to change it. In some cases, a white candle and a glass of water may be enough to offer a practitioner peace, calm, and the clarity to bring about positive change; in other instances, bigger offerings must be used. Only divination can help someone discern the difference.

CHAPTER NINE
VOODOO AND LUCUMÍ RELIGIOUS RITUALS

In Voodoo, Vodou, and Lucumí traditions, almost all actions are seen as having a sacred significance and could arguably be considered ritual. In some iles, even the simple act of turning around is considered sacred and must be performed in a certain way. For people who are used to practicing their religion only once a week or once a year, this level of dedication is often difficult to process. This chapter will deal with group and solitary rituals, both public and private.

RITUAL PRACTICES

In addition to looking different from your average non-ATR practitioner, the rituals, spells, and experience of Voodoo and Lucumí are also different. Simple cleansings are done with items like cigars and rum, which can be used at the start of a ceremony or whenever needed. The cigar smoke and/or rum is sprayed and blown around the area to remove negativity and open the path for progress and expansion.

In the African Traditional Religions, ritual has a basic structure, but practitioners know that everything leading up to the ceremony, and also everything that comes after, is a necessary and sacred part of the process. Space and time operate differently here. That is not to say there are not boundaries, because the ritual area will be apparent. If all is going properly, the unnecessary or uninvited energies both natural and supernatural will meet with a strong psychic barrier. Sacred Geometry is experienced on a whole other level. The spiritual containment lines will have been laid by the mambo and houngan or Santero and Santera, and the rest of their congregation. Participants have loosely defined roles during the actual ritual. Individuals may be designated as drummers or dancers, but that role could shift at any moment and should not be adhered to rigidly. The hounfor or ile operates like a supportive family, with people providing complementary assistance to accomplish the tasks at hand. The tasks during ritual most likely involve honoring the Lwa or Orisha. The invitations to these divinities are done through drumming, dancing, and chanting, all orchestrated by the spiritual elders present. In most cases, the drum rhythms, songs, and dance movements have been in use for decades if not centuries. At the end of a ceremony there is no "farewell." The Lwa and Orisha always come and go as they please, and the close of a ritual for them is more like the end of a party when you turn on the lights and find that most of the people have gone home. People who are under the influence of trance-possession can display extreme physical powers. They have been known to perform a wide range of feats. For example, I once watched a priestess roll across hot coals. Even though much of what occurs seems fantastical, there is little to no effect on the body of the possessed person. It is almost as if the traditional laws of nature do not apply in this situation. These amazing events are, in part, used to signal the presence of the Lwa or Orisha. If the spiritual family witnesses a 4½-foot-tall mambo pick up a 300-pound man and spin him around, they are assured they are in the presence of the Lwa. As a ritual proceeds, often lasting for several hours, participants begin to discover a new way of understanding and functioning.

Newcomers, however, also need to realize that ATR practitioners do not use the same methods of grounding and centering as other religions. Florida Water is a magickal water used for spiritual cleansing and protection, and it is used during ceremonies to stabilize participants. It is available in many large supermarkets in the ethnic food and products section, or it can be obtained online. In Lucumí, Florida Water, as well as cascarilla, can be used for similar purposes. They are sprinkled over or applied to the person or area in question.

GROUP RITUAL

The large public group ritual is the type of spiritual worship that most beginners are likely to encounter. Voodoo and other ATR rituals have recently become more open to outsiders and are even taking place at gatherings and events. I've attended rituals everywhere from universities to art galleries. My own spiritual house, the House of Maman Brigitte, even performed the closing ritual for NYC Pagan Pride. Many of the larger spiritual houses of African Traditional Religion have frequent ceremonies that are open to respectful members of the general public. These ceremonies run from simple bembes to more elaborate extravaganzas for initiations like the Vodou Lavé Tet.

Public Ancestor ritual by Lilith Dorsey and House of Maman Brigitte in Sleepy Hollow. – [photo by author]

Most large public rituals of this type will include a primary altar area or table for offerings of food and drink, flowers, money, herbs, and candles. There are also several supporting altar areas; for example, there may be a separate ritual altar area set up near the drummers or dancers. There can also be altars set up to honor certain Lwa or Orisha who do not wish to "sit" at the table with others; for example, Oyá and Oshún are never put near each other. These two Orisha do not get along, as they both fought over their relationship with Changó. I even attended one ceremony where dozens of tables were set up with offerings, such as alcohol and cigarettes, for participants to use during the ritual. In traditional forms of Haitian

Vodou, the shrine is frequently set up on the earth around what is called a poteau mitan (center pole). A vévé is also laid on the earth around the center pole as a spiritual conduit for the Lwa to travel through and across. The ritual dancers then proceed to carry sacred flags across this vévé while dancing. Sometimes, this will be followed by a series of trance-possession events by various Lwa. Participants are never sure which Lwa are going to appear and are frequently surprised. When the Lwa descend, the possessed persons frequently speak Haitian Creole or other ancestral languages (even if they have never spoken them before), dance, sing, and offer messages for the community and individuals.

In the New Orleans Voodoo tradition, large group rituals are similar to the Haitian type of ritual but also work hard to include multicultural elements. At the Voodoo Spiritual Temple in New Orleans, there are always temple members and visitors who come from a variety of backgrounds. Consequently, efforts are made to learn from these other religions.

By contrast, La Regla Lucumí can be seen as having a more traditional and codified set of practices surrounding its group rituals. For over 300 years, every effort has been made by Santería practitioners to preserve the traditions in the manner in which they were started back in West Africa. That is not to say there is no variation within the religion. Each ile does things in its own particularly unique way; however, a ritual given by a Santera today may look surprisingly a lot like one that may have been given by her spiritual parents and grandparents 50 or 100 years earlier. At their core, each ritual has a basic order of service.

Order of Service for Public Group Ritual

Each order of service is particular to the individual spiritual house and situation. Most often, however, the first Orisha to be honored will be Elegguá in a Lucumí ceremony or Legba in a Vodou ceremony. The ritual will begin with songs, chants, calls, and drum rhythms for Elegguá or Legba (known as Eshú in Ifá and Papa Lebat in New Orleans). In each tradition, this divinity is responsible for opening doors and roads and removing unnecessary obstacles. Elegguá and Legba provide guidance and function as a messenger between the physical world of the participants and the spiritual world of the Lwa or Orisha.

Whatever order follows from this point is determined by the priest and priestess and the Lwa or Orisha themselves. Very likely Ogou, also known as Ogún, will be honored next with military-style drumbeats, regimented movements, and a machete or some form of iron. Depending on the situation, he is called to heal and protect the community, as well as to clear the spiritual path to victory. Ogou is symbolically responsible for clearing away the blockages on one's proper path.

The next Lwa or Orisha to be given service will be the one who is the primary focus of the ceremony. If it is a feast or ceremony to honor a certain Orisha, such as Oshún, now would be the time the drum rhythms for her would begin, and offerings of food, particularly honey, would be given. Participants are now called on to dance, and Oshún's favorite songs are sung, praising her beauty and grace. The aim here is to achieve a level of union with the Orisha; this could be through trance-possession, which will provide contact with the Lwa or Orisha on a direct level and will also allow the Lwa to experience again through a human body, or it can just be through a feeling of ashé that radiates through participants. The ceremony then continues, sometimes for hours, until the priest, priestess, and divinities feel the ritual is complete.

Order of Service for Private Group Ritual

Private group ritual in the African Traditional Religions is similar to the public ritual. The major difference that I have seen is in the scale and format of the ceremony. Private group rituals can be smaller, consisting of less than 25 dedicated members of the ile. I can only liken it to the difference between a meal at home and a meal in a restaurant. An ile or hounfor is a family, and the bonds contained within it are strong and focused. Each individual has a function and place, and it is within these smaller private rituals that they are able to recharge and work with their family to achieve their goals.

A Typical Order of Service for a Private Group Ritual for Marie Laveau, the Voodoo Queen of New Orleans

Bamboula drum rhythm is played as a call to service. Originating in Africa, this rhythm and accompanying dance of resistance have been popular for hundreds of years. This will help to gather and focus the participants in attendance. Next will be the rhythm for Papa Legba/ Lebat, the New Orleans Voodoo gatekeeper responsible for allowing the ceremony to occur. Offerings can and do include coffee, cigars, money, coconut, rum and/or gin, and candy. Laughter and bizarre backward happenings will frequently signal his presence. Call and rhythm for Ogún will be the next segment of the ritual. Offerings consist of rum, cigars, clanging metal or knives, and blood or red palm oil. The next part of the ceremony will include words of love, praise, and prayers to Marie Laveau. Most likely, the Yanvalou rhythm will be played, and a snake (if one is available) will be brought out to move and interact with the participants. Offerings of sweet cakes, champagne, cigarettes, money, holy water (as Laveau was also a devout Catholic), and salt water are made.

Most of the smaller private rituals I have attended are more flexible than their larger counterparts. Because of the smaller and more intense nature of the rituals, participants are able to interact with the Lwa or Orisha more directly. Frequently, private group rituals are occasions for initiations. These can only be described as being similar to birth. Much work and labor go into the creation of a new and different person. It is ultimately an occasion for great joy.

SOLITARY RITUAL

Solitary ritual practices occur several times a day for most followers of African Traditional Religions. These rituals very often include candle magick, ritual baths and floor washes, offerings of money or other items, incense-burning, and prayer.

Initiates in these traditions are each given their own personal set of ritual tasks to be carried out daily, monthly, or as needed. For example, a son or daughter of Oyá could be required to travel to the cemetery to leave offerings every Wednesday, keep an eternal flame dedicated to the goddess on his or her altar, and/or never eat eggplant—one of Oyá's ritual foods. Each of these ritual requirements is determined by complex layers of divination by elders in the religion.

The uninitiated are very limited in the solitary rituals they can perform. These are religions with sacred knowledge and practices that can only be learned through repeated contact with a qualified priestess and/or priest. Some level of initiation is required for almost all serious practice.

One of the things that anyone can do, however, is set up an ancestor altar or shrine, which is discussed in chapter 7. It is a wonderful way to begin contact with those who have gone before, and I recommend it for anyone, whether he or she is interested in African Traditional Religions or not.

Creating a Magickal Journal

Another spiritual tool that the solitary can create is a Lwa or Orisha journal. This magickal journal is a place to record contact with the divine. If you wish to discover more about your proper spiritual path while you sleep, place a small bowl of water underneath your bed. Hopefully, this will catch any negativity in the area that could be affecting your sleep. Begin by burning a small amount of Seven African Powers incense or Elegguá incense. To the best of your ability, remove all distractions and calm your mind. Sprinkle your sleeping area with Florida Water to bring you peace and clarity. Then, with your magickal notebook and writing implements within reach, go to sleep. If you wish to learn more about a particular Lwa or Orisha, concentrate on the image of his or her vévé in your mind or place it under your pillow on a piece of parchment paper. When you wake, record all that you can remember in your journal. In addition to these dreams, you can record any other spiritual experiences or manifestations. Some practitioners believe that contact with a Lwa or Orisha can be observed even in the simplest forms around us. For example, a son of Changó might have things like apples, patchouli, turtles, and other favored offerings present in his environment more than usual. Your journal is the place to record unusual contacts with animals, plants, and people. Review your journal periodically to see if there are any recurring themes or trends that could indicate the direction in which your spiritual path is headed. Then seek proper guidance, and maybe even divination, with a trusted elder.

A Ritual of Transformation

This next ritual is designed to familiarize people with the process of Voodoo transformation. The following working is to bring clarity and a higher consciousness similar to that which occurs during ritual with a Lwa or Orisha. First, make sure your environment is physically and spiritually clean. Use magickal floor wash preparations from a botanica or online. Burn white seven-day candles (until the glass burns clean and clear) in the days and hours leading up to the working. Clear a 4-by-4-foot (or larger) area in which to perform the rite. Find someone to be your watcher, to make sure you have spiritual backup. Explain to him or her what you are attempting, and instruct him or her to cleanse the back of your neck with cascarilla and/or Florida Water. They should repeat this anytime it looks like you are having an unpleasant experience and would like to return to your body. Put on some ritual drum music. The sounds will assist and guide you on your journey to other realms. Draw a véve of the crossroads for Papa Legba on the floor in cornmeal and stand barefoot in the center. Remember: You are not trying to invoke or petition but are merely reaching out and greeting the ashé with respect and reverence.

Feel the corn under your feet and try your best to still your mind. If you feel the need, you can move or dance to the music. The simple box step is a good way to free up your body. Continue this until you feel a change in the atmosphere surrounding you. You may feel giddy or dizzy, the background may start to recede, and your focus may begin to shift. Pay attention to how all is changing slightly. When you feel you have had enough, signal your assistant to cleanse your body, paying special attention to the hands, feet, and back of the neck. After everything is finished, be sure to record your experiences and discuss them with your spiritual teachers.

CHAPTER TEN

VOODOO ON THE SILVER SCREEN

Dancing beneath the moon, ecstatic, frenzied communications with gods, cemeteries, chicken feet, swamps, and handling serpents are all images that belong to the Voodoo world of cinema and television. The filmic depictions of Voodoo and Santería run the gamut from *Madame Satan* (1930) to more modern representations such as *Daughters of the Dust* (1991), *Eve's Bayou* (1997), and *In Search of Voodoo: Roots to Heaven* (2018).

Unfortunately, Voodoo is most frequently portrayed on film as a wild African holdover that is simultaneously strange, evil, sexual, and perverse. Only in a few instances is it shown on screen as a positive element. It is in these glimpses we see part of the true nature of the religion that manifests as powerful, ancestral, or a possible economic alternative.

Voodoo on the screen provides the viewers with a whole subset of BIPOC stereotypes. They form a patchwork—a virtual, cinematic Voodoo Tarot—that is full of archetypal characters. Branching out from the usual screen mammies and Uncle Toms, we find here crazy root women, conjure men, nefarious divinities, and walking dead. They function, in the same way, however, to provide one-dimensional representations that often marginalize and degrade African Americans. Even *Jezebel*, the great southern classic, features a line where Henry Fonda says, "I am a banker, not a conjure man," implying these men were often dealing in the realm of the spiritual as opposed to practical.

Madame Satan (1930)
Directed by Cecil B. DeMille
Cast: Kay Johnson, Reginald Denny

The theme of White-against-Black Voodoo is one that is revisited throughout the films dealing with Voodoo. One of the earliest instances of this is

Madame Satan. It features a group of African American men on the street corner shooting craps and discussing Hoodoo, the herbal-based form of African Traditional Religion. The scene plays out with the men saying they are not afraid of hoodoos or anything, when an alabaster-skinned beauty dressed in white parachutes into their game and sends them screaming for their lives.

The Green Pastures (1936)
Directed by Marc Connelly and William Keighley
Cast: Rex Ingram, Oscar Polk

Billed as a fable by Marc Connelly and William Keighley and based on Roark Bradford's *Ol' Man Adam and his Chillun'*, the Black extravaganza *The Green Pastures* premiered in 1936. The film's patronizing desire to explain the religious life of African Americans is delineated in the film's foreword, "Thousands of Negroes in the deep South visualize

God and heaven in terms of people and things they know in their everyday life. *The Green Pastures* is an attempt to portray that humble reverent conception."

The film goes on to show all-Black versions of several classic Bible stories, which systematically denounce various ATR practices. Many African-based practices are denounced in this film. It systematically provides loose Christian reasoning for abandoning various African practices that could be associated with religions such as Voodoo. One scene features a declaration from a dark-skinned God, "Tell them from now on dancing around the moon is sinning." An extended episode toward the end of the movie pits holy men against the Voodoo "boys [with] the gris-gris."

The Green Pastures also touches on the sexual practices of the Voodoo-worshipping Blacks of the South. In one scene, the angel Gabriel remarks, "That's the village with the fortune-tellers. They certainly can breed fast"—again, the implication being that Voodoo functions as a watershed for lascivious sexual practices. This film blatantly shows the kind of racism and prejudice that existed at the time.

Stormy Weather (1943)
Directed by Andrew L. Stone

Cast: Katherine Dunham, Fayard Nicholas, Harold Nicholas, Lena Horne, Bill Robinson, Cab Calloway

In this film, the lead character, Bill Williamson (played by Bill Robinson) reminisces about his colorful past in the entertainment industry. The cast is a cavalcade of great African American entertainers who worked in an era when their lives were stymied by racism and oppression. Of particular note is the wonderful title dance number for the goddess of lightning and the storm choreographed by the anthropologist and

Vodou initiate Katherine Dunham. This number consists of a sinuous and flowing dance piece grounded in the roots of Vodou practice.

Divine Horseman: The Living Gods of Haiti (1951, RELEASED 1985)
Directed by Maya Deren

This film is the culmination of the anthropological fieldwork done by Maya Deren in Haiti. She shot several hours of footage, and it was not edited and released until after her death. The film does a marvelous job of presenting both the sacred and beautiful nature of the practices in Haiti. As an experimental filmmaker, Deren was able to visually represent the divine dance of trance-possession.

Live and Let Die (1973)
Directed by Guy Hamilton

Cast: Roger Moore, Jane Seymour, Yaphet Kotto, Geoffrey Holder

In this film our hero is James Bond, who battles Caribbean drug dealers in both New York and on the islands. In *Live and Let Die*, the Vodou takes place underneath a thin veil of normalcy. Bond in this film frequently runs into Vodou happenings in bars, stores, hotels, and so on. Even the Bond Girl of this film, Solitaire (Jane Seymour), practices the religion meeting with only playful disdain. Orgiastic Vodou ritual is also featured in this classic Bond feature. The final ritual scene employs scantily clad dancers preparing to offer up Solitaire, in see-through white chiffon, for sacrifice. Choreographed by Geoffrey Holder, who also plays the Baron

Samedi, the dance and ritual portions of the film show a surprising degree of authenticity. There are rumors that Holder may have been an ATR practitioner himself. Retentions of Creole language and a few genuine ritual gestures hopefully distract from the rubber snakes and Seymour's nipples. In *Live and Let Die*, it is Bond himself who foils the Voodooists who are attempting to sacrifice Solitaire. Bond spies on the ceremony with his own unique version of the perverse gaze. He then quickly makes his move to blow the life out of Baron Samedi.

Within the economically marginalized communities of African Americans in the southern United States and the Caribbean, Voodoo and Vodou have always served as viable money-generating alternatives. It was a profitable solution to a difficult problem, particularly for African American women, who often performed in real life and on film as domestics and caretakers.

The end of this film sees Bond foil the evil dead and make the world safe again. Films like these set up a polemic where, if good can only thwart the evil of Vodou, the problems of drugs and crime will disappear. This is an entertaining piece of fantasy, but not much more can be said about it.

Amulet of Ogum (1974)
aka Amuleto de Ogum
Directed by Nelson Pereira dos Santos
Cast: Ney Santanna, Anecy Rocha, Jofre Soares, Jards Macalé, Maria Ribeiro

This film depicts an underworld full of Umbanda, Candomblé, crime, and tragedy. To entertain some thieves, a blind guitar player recounts the story of a man from northeast Brazil, who was involved with gangsters and living in the suburbs of Rio de Janeiro. This man had a "closed body"—meaning that his body couldn't be hit by bullets or other weapons—by the wish of Ogum, the god of war and iron. I highly recommend this film if you can find it.

Sugar Hill (1974)
aka The Zombies of Sugar Hill and Voodoo Girl
Directed by Paul Maslansky

Tagline: "Meet Sugar Hill and her Zombie Hit Men ... The Mafia has never met anything like them!"

Cast: Marki Bey, Don Pedro Colley, Robert Quarry, Richard Lawson, Zara Cully, Betty Anne Rees, Charles Robinson

This film is a cult classic. The plot is predicated on a contractual agreement between the heroine, Diana "Sugar" Hill, and the Voodoo god Baron Samedi. The Baron asks to be paid for his services with sexual favors. Traditionally, the Baron is associated with sex and lewd behavior, as well as the named dead. *Sugar Hill* sexualizes several aspects of Voodoo during the film. This screen version extrapolates these notions to provide this Baron with zombie wives dressed in thin lingerie. The end of the film has Sugar Hill agree to repay her debt by offering up the white girlfriend of her nemesis. The Baron reluctantly agrees to take the substitute on a temporary basis, again stressing the cinematic "importance" of sex in the world of Voodoo.

Sugar Hill provides a classic 1974 Blaxploitation treatment of the religion of Voodoo. At its core is the revenge of driven vigilante protagonist Sugar Hill, who uses the power of Baron Samedi to fight evil white criminals. The film provides a rare look at a scenario in which the white characters in the film are seen as the evil ones, and Voodoo—while containing extreme methods—provides our heroine with a vigilante form of justice.

Xe do Caixão (Coffin Joe) series of three films

Directed and written by José Mojica Marins; these films include:

Ritual dos Sádicos, O (1970) aka *Awakening of the Beast* (UK) and *Ritual of the Maniacs (U.S.)*

Exorcismo Negro, O (1974) aka *Black Exorcism of Coffin Joe* and *The Bloody Exorcism of Coffin Joe*

A Estranha Hospedaria dos Prazeres (1976) aka *The Strange Hostel of Naked Pleasures*

These Brazilian horror films are some of the best ever made. They focus on the exploits of Coffin Joe, an angry undertaker who seeks revenge on those who cross his path. The concept of the divine in Afro-Atlantic tradition is based on worship and patronage of an individual, usually after he or she is deceased. After the *Coffin Joe* films were released, many Brazilians began to worship the character as an Orixa of the dead. In the case of Coffin Joe, a wide variety of factors contributed to his cult status and semi-deification as a spirit of the ancestors and the energy of the dead. Filmmaker José Mojica Marins mentions that several times while they were filming in cemeteries at night, they came across an Umbanda or Candomblé ritual. The participants frequently became extras in the films. These films are freaky and not for the weak-stomached, but I do recommend them as some of the strangest movies you will ever see.

Dona Flor e Seus Dois Maridos (1976)
aka Dona Flor and Her Two Husbands
Directed by Bruno Barreto

Cast: Sonja Braga, José Wilker, Mauro Mendonça, Dinorah Brillanti

This film is set in Bahia, Brazil, and tells the story of Flor, a woman caught between a living husband and a dead one. Here the reality of the ancestor spirits is brought to the fore. This is the cinematic adaptation of Jorge Amado's bestselling book of the same name. Amado himself held the title of Obá in the religion. All of Amado's stories artfully represent the practices of the religion of Candomblé, and this film is no exception.

Legacy of the Spirits (1985)
Directed by Karen Kramer

This fantastic documentary delves into the world of African Diasporic Religion as it is practiced in New York City. My own Vodou godmother, Bonnie Devlin, even has a cameo appearance drumming in the film. This is one of the best documentaries available on Vodou in the Diaspora. Karen Kramer was at New York University film school just before I was, and she does a wonderful job of presenting a complex subject.

Something Wild (1986)
Directed by Jonathan Demme

Cast: Jeff Daniels, Ray Liotta, Melanie Griffith

Melanie Griffith and Jeff Daniels star in this strange road movie from director Jonathan Demme. Charlie Driggs (Daniels) is a shy New York investment broker who lets himself be abducted during his lunch hour by an attractive eccentric named Audrey Hankel (Griffith). While drunk, she drives him to a hotel for some kinky sex and minor thievery, and eventually convinces him to accompany her and pretend to be her husband at her high school reunion. Charlie finds himself loosening up and falling in love, but then the film makes a sudden left turn with the appearance of Ray (played by Ray Liotta), Hankel's ex-con husband. There are a number of cameo appearances that include directors John Waters and John Sayles.

So often, Voodoo and its resulting practices are viewed as a hidden, unseemly part of Black culture. It exists beyond the sight of the average member of society, and its followers are viewed as, to borrow a term from anthropology, repugnant cultural others.

An instance of "repugnant cultural others" surfacing on the silver screen is Demme's film. Incorporating a quirky southern gothic style and extended scenes in Virginia, the film has Griffith as a Voodoo practitioner with a complex system of beliefs and several warrants for her arrest. Yet, it is not the almost-omnipresent elements of the religion that are considered strange, for Daniels' character's abandonment of normalcy is considered the wild act. His desire to be with a woman as wild as Griffith is portrayed as the ultimate folly. This movie is interesting to watch, but I do not appreciate its overall portrayal of Voodoo practitioners.

Angel Heart (1987)
Directed by Alan Parker
Cast: Mickey Rourke, Lisa Bonet, Robert De Niro, Charlotte Rampling, Stocker Fontelieu

When most people think of a New Orleans Voodoo film, they think *Angel Heart*. The plot of this film centers around Harry Angel (Mickey Rourke), a 1950s detective hired by a dark stranger to search for the man responsible for a string of horrific murders leading from New York to the Voodoo cults of New Orleans. Angel quickly encounters the exotic Voodoo queen Epiphany Proudfoot, artfully portrayed by Lisa Bonet.

Proudfoot is highly sexualized despite her young age of 17. The scene in *Angel Heart* that most directly links Voodoo with hypersexuality is the main ritual scene. Staged by Parker's longtime choreographer Louis Falco, whom he employed in the film *Fame*, the scene features a ritual that employs few of the traditional Voodoo elements. From there it quickly degenerates into a half-naked debacle with a dead chicken, reminiscent of Falco's "Hot Lunch" dance number in *Fame*. Falco, however, believes the scene is representative of an "authentic ritual ceremony." The dancers are primarily "professionals from New York." This oxymoronic logic is the type that is frequently employed by the creators of negative media conceptions of Voodoo. Another cinematic trope is depicted in the form of the Voodoo shop. Like *Live and Let Die*'s Oh Cult Voodoo Shop, the Voodoo shop here (Mammy Carter's) features a powerful, sassy Black woman as its proprietress. The commodification of the religion is an element that definitely carries over to the screen.

Voodoo, the religion of the mostly nameless, faceless African Americans in the film, is set up in opposition to the evil of Satanism, the practice of almost all the whites in the film. Although based on William Hjortsberg's novel *Fallen Angel*, which never leaves New York State, Parker chooses to move his tale to New Orleans. This movie looks good, but the Voodoo is wholeheartedly melodramatic.

The Believers (1987)
Directed by John Schlesinger
Tagline: "They exist. Fear them."
Cast: Martin Sheen, Robert Loggia, Jimmy Smits, Carla Pinza

Martin Sheen is a New York psychiatrist who finds that a Voodoo cult, which practices child sacrifice, has an interest in his own son. Sheen battles the hidden "evils" of Santería and Voodoo in this film. Bloody fetishes and unnecessary violence run throughout this film. There is nothing realistic or of amusement value in this film.

Voodoo Dawn (1990)
Directed by Steven Fierberg
Tagline: "If you thought voodoo was mumbo jumbo, it's time to think again."
Cast: Raymond St. Jacques, Theresa Merritt, Gina Gershon, Tony Todd

A group of immigrant Haitian farm workers, with the assistance of a caring anthropology student, tries to fight off an evil Haitian Voodoo priest in this ridiculous film. *Voodoo Dawn* has the white lead character in the position of being the only one who can save the poor unfortunate Voodoo practitioners from the evil agent of their own religion. One wonders why the other African American characters put their faith in this man, who has recently arrived from up North and is ignorant of all Voodoo practices. Revenge is the motive for the evil Voodoo elements depicted in this film. In this case, it is a former soldier of the Tonton Macoute, the Haitian secret police, who comes to enact vengeance on the displaced Voodoo practitioners in the Louisiana bayou. This film isn't worth the celluloid it was printed on.

Daughters of the Dust (1991)
Directed by Julie Dash
Cast: Cora Lee Day, Adisa Anderson, Alva Rogers,
Bahni Turpin, Kaycee Moore, Trula Hoosier
Winner of the Award for Best Cinematography at the Sundance Film Festival

Julie Dash's critically acclaimed *Daughters of the Dust* provides several characters who turn toward ATR's power. The story chronicles the tale of the Peazant family, a family with a history intrinsically linked to the spiritual beliefs of Africa. The power of the Orisha and the ancestors working through the Ibo people in South Carolina is one of the central themes of the film. The Ibo myth, as it relates to Ibo Point in South Carolina, concerns the African slaves of the Ibo tribe who were brought to America. They refused to live in slavery, and many walked straight into the water at a place called Ibo Point. Some say they drowned; some say they flew all the way back to Africa. Their descendants today are still called "the flying Ibo people," and it is these people whom Dash profiles in the film.

Daughters of the Dust even extends the influence of the Orisha and the religion to the musical score. The original score was crafted by John Barnes, and the closing theme is called "Elegba Theme." Elegba, also known as Legba or Eleggúa, is the Voodoo guardian of the crossroads. The lyrics petition Elegba, "Ago Elegba ... show the way, Elegba." It is this crossroads-dwelling divinity Elegba who grants wishes and provides contact with the spirit world. Elegba is one Orisha directly represented in *Daughters of the Dust*. Elegba is invoked in the character of the unborn child. Nana Peazant in *Daughters of the Dust* plays the interesting Hoodoo woman role. The script notes list her as being equal to Obatalá, the African deity for peace and calm, embodying the energy of the clouds and often petitioned by the mentally ill.

Thankfully, *Daughters of the Dust* gives cinema one of the truest portrayals of Voodoo as ancestral legacy. It is here that we see the wisdom of the ancestors as inseparable from the religion of Voodoo. Dash comments that many of her family's own stories were the basis for the film, making it a testament to her own reverence for ancestral knowledge and tradition. The film is set in the Sea Islands of South Carolina. It seems that ancestor reverence, if not worship, is alive and well, and not just among the Voodoo practitioners.

Raw Footage (1927-1940)
Directed and written by Zora Neale Hurston

Zora Neale Hurston was the first African American woman to get her anthropology degree from Barnard College. During the late 1920s and early 1940s, she filmed several different scenes of African American religious life throughout the southern United States. The footage includes a Lucumí style Rogación (water baptism) that takes place off the Florida coast, and a Vodou drumming ceremony in South Carolina. The footage is a rare archival document, possibly the earliest film ever of practices like these in the United States. Unfortunately, when I first wrote this book, the only place to see the footage was in the Library of Congress. Thanks to the work of myself and other devoted scholars, it was made available to the public.

Midnight in the Garden of Good and Evil (1997)
Directed by Clint Eastwood
Cast: **John Cusack, Kevin Spacey, Jack Thompson, Irma P. Hall, Jude Law, Alison Eastwood, Paul Hipp, The Lady Chablis, Dorothy Loudon**

Midnight in the Garden of Good and Evil is the story of a wealthy Charleston man who kills his male lover. The film follows the man through the trial as seen by a journalist, played by John Cusack.

There are several scenes in *Midnight in the Garden of Good and Evil* that feature typical Hoodoo and Voodoo practices. Consistent with the rest of the film, these scenes are a bit sensationalist. It does, however, give a relatively accurate portrayal of the kinds of spells some people perform. Not everyone is at a murder victim's graveside at midnight as part of their religion, but things like this can occur, and sometimes Voodoo and Hoodoo are a person's only option.

Eve's Bayou (1997)
Directed by Kasi Lemmons
Tagline: "The secrets that hold us together can also tear us apart."
Cast: Jurnee Smollett, Meagan Good, Samuel L. Jackson, Lynn Whitfield, Debbi Morgan, Ethel Ayler, Diahann Carroll, Vondie Curtis-Hall, Branford Marsalis

This story is set in 1962 Louisiana and chronicles the Batiste family through the eyes of their daughter, Eve. They live in a world of intrigue and mysticism, and this coming-of-age story has a depth and a warmth that one rarely finds when dealing with the subject of Hoodoo and the other ATRs.

In *Eve's Bayou*, the unstable Hoodoo woman Elzora is portrayed by Diahann Carroll. Depicted as unclean and rambling, mad Elzora evokes an age-old stereotype regarding the religion of Hoodoo and psychic phenomena in general. The performance is hidden under a profuse amount of whiteface makeup, intended to be evocative of Yoruba ancestor markings. Here, the audience sees character drift into ominous caricature. Elzora lives amid jars of herbs and homunculi in the wild swamps, conjuring during the wee hours of the night and bringing death and tragedy. Kasi Lemmons' association of her with Hoodoo, as opposed to Voodoo, offers an interesting insight into the character. Hoodoo as a tradition is seen to be more independent, less formalized, and dependent on an intimate knowledge of herbal pharmacology.

In *Eve's Bayou*, the function Hoodoo plays slowly shifts from helpful insight into the future and useful herbal potions to problematic agent of death. Eve enlists the help of Elzora to bring about the death of her father. Eve is determined to punish her father for various improprieties and goes to great lengths to bring about his demise.

Eve's Bayou begins with the main character setting the stage for the psychic component of the film. Eve explains, "Like others before me, I have the gift of sight." The gift of second sight obviously runs in the Batiste family as it is also a talent of Eve's aunt, Mozelle. Lemmons gives us the rare opportunity to view Hoodoo as an everyday component of life among the Black communities of Louisiana she is portraying. Like Eve's red hair, Hoodoo is portrayed as a genetic trait that some are fortunate enough to possess.

In *Eve's Bayou*, the power of Hoodoo also provides an undercurrent for the film. Mozelle, played by Debbi Morgan, earns her living from psychic readings. Her power to foretell events helps members of the African American community. Mozelle also displays a knowledge of Hoodoo roots and herbs. From her sacred box she pulls ingredients for a traditional Hoodoo gris-gris containing lodestone, Hi John the Conqueror root, devil's shoestring, and holy water. Even though Mozelle receives ridicule from her family, she is still seen as possessing a gift that she uses for economic gain. We see a constant parade of customers in and out of her home, seeking guidance, information, and potions, and consequently leaving appropriate donations. The nefarious character Elzora also earns her living through Hoodoo with a small vending shack, where she sells her odd bits and does bone readings, a Louisiana standard. She taps her hand on a jar filled with dollar bills, and the reality of her situation is made clear.

In contrast to all the negative and flawed depictions of the African Diasporic Religion of Hoodoo, it is also often portrayed in the media as an undeniable power. Functioning as an empowering option for the frequently marginalized African American, the potent spells and abilities of Hoodoo still find their way into these films. It is also interesting to note that this was the first feature-length studio film directed by a Black woman. Lemmons went on to direct *Harriet*, about Harriet Tubman, in 2019.

Blues Brothers 2000 (1998)
Directed by **John Landis**
Tagline: "The Lord works in mysterious ways."
Cast: **Dan Aykroyd, John Goodman, Erykah Badu, Nia Peeples, B. B. King, Eric Clapton, Dr. John**

The plot of this film has Elwood Blues (Dan Aykroyd) trying to reunite his band for one last big show. Erykah Badu portrays the Voodoo Queen Mousette in *Blues Brothers 2000*. Here, the dark-suited Blues Brothers clan comes up against the Voodoo Queen, calling her the "ugliest, oldest, and meanest Voodoo witch." Despite their reluctance, they approach Mousette's "Plantation Club" to ask for an audition. She responds with kindness and a song, and a bit of stereotypical zombification thrown in. Their temporary zombification can be seen as a displacement of their fears concerning Voodoo. They are improved musically through the power of Voodoo yet still remain at a safe distance from Queen Mousette. The best part of the film is the closing number featuring a cavalcade of stars in the band "Louisiana Gator Boys." Here we see such giants as BB King, Eric Clapton, Bo Diddley, and my dear friend Dr. John.

Miel para Oshún (2001)
aka Honey for Oshún
Directed by Humberto Solás
Cast: Jorge Perugorría, Isabel Santos, Mario Limonta, Saturnino Garcia, Adela Legrá

When his father dies, a Cuban man who was raised in the United States learns that he was not abandoned by his mother but instead was taken illegally out of Cuba. He returns to the island and is helped in his search by a cousin and a taxi driver. The Orisha Oshún becomes a metaphor for both his lost mother and his lost homeland. There are several beautiful images of Cuba in this film and a small amount of information about the La Regla Lucumí practices there.

City of God (2002)
aka Cidade de Deus
Directed by Fernando Meirelles and Katia Lund
Tagline: "Fight and you'll never survive ... Run and you'll never escape."
Cast: Alexandre Rodrigues, Leandro Firmino, Phellipe Haagensen, Douglas Silva, Jonathan Haagensen, Matheus Nachtergaele

This visually brilliant and emotionally gripping film has a steady undercurrent of Candomblé practices. It presents the reality of the violent *favelas* (shantytowns on the city's edge) in Brazil. The film is based on the real-life story of a young photographer trying to find a way out of the misery that is all around him. Candomblé elements run throughout the film, functioning as a catalyst for change.

Bodies of Water. – [photo by author]

Bodies of Water: Voodoo Identity and Transformation (2004)
Directed by Lilith Dorsey

Shot shortly before Hurricane Katrina, this is my own documentary look at the sacred religion of New Orleans Voodoo. Paramount in the New Orleans Voodoo tradition is a connection to the Mississippi River and Lake Pontchartrain as interconnected sites of spiritual healing and growth. In this film, people are represented as connected to this elemental power, constantly changing and adapting like the waterways they mimic, providing guidance, direction, and nourishment.

Brooklyn to Benin: A Vodou Pilgrimage (2016)
Directed by Regine Romain

Romain is a phenomenal director, and this is one of the few documentaries to come out in recent years that truly shows the face of the sacred religion. The film shows practices around the globe from Brooklyn to Haiti to Benin as the title states.

In Search of Voodoo: Roots to Heaven (2018)
Directed by Djimon Hounsou

This film is the creation of actor/director Djimon Hounsou. Using phenomenal imagery and first-person accounts, Hounsou documents the religion in his home country of Benin as only he can. Of particular note are the amazing scenes of rituals for Mami Wata.

Harriet (2019)
Directed by Kasi Lemmons
Starring: Cynthia Erivo, Janelle Monáe, Leslie Odom Jr.

Iconic Underground Railroad freedom fighter Harriet Tubman is chronicled in this film. The spiritual scenes in the film were loosely framed and experimental. While this film met with controversy, Harriet Tubman was and is an inspiration foremother to so many of us. Her story needs to be told and remembered. My hope is that will turn more people's attention to this amazing woman. For those wishing to discover more about the magick of Harriet Tubman, I highly recommend Witchdoctor Utu's book, *Conjuring Harriet "Mama Moses" Tubman and the Spirits of the Underground Railroad*.

Roll Credits

Voodoo in the cinema is often shown as backward, dangerous, wild, and feared, and yet it continues despite these (and many more) misconceptions. This ancient African religion has suffered and resisted, existing on film in many different ways and engaging many different issues—issues that are especially valuable when considering the religions as a whole.

One particular current that I feel is directly revealed when we look at these films is the role of Black women. Pioneers like Katherine Dunham and Zora Neale Hurston sought out the practices to document and explore them. In doing so, they found strength and beauty that they were able to bring to the world. Directors like Kasi Lemmons and Julie Dash also found strength in these images of women in power. Continuing to manifest in real life and on the silver screen as strong, profitable, and ancestral, it seems that Voodoo, in the words of Cary Grant, "got the power."

CHAPTER ELEVEN
BLACK ROOTS TO LIVE BY
ROOT MAGICK FOR PROTECTION AND PROTEST

By definition, the African Traditional Religion is Black Magick. Not some dark magick filled with evil, but magick traditionally done by and for Black people. For over 400 years it has been magick for resistance and utilized absolutely everything it had at its disposal. Despite the large number of years that have passed, the need for protection and protest magick is as great as ever. Recent times have witnessed police killings of an alarming number of Black people including Breonna Taylor, Rayshard Brooks, Daniel Prude, Atatiana Jefferson, Aura Rosser, Stephon Clark, Botham Jean, Philando Castille, Alton Sterling, Michelle Cusseaux, Freddie Gray, Janisha Fonville, Eric Garner, Akai Gurley, Gabriella Nevarez, George Floyd, and many others. Voting rights in the U.S. have been eroded to pre-Civil-Rights-era levels, and the country has continued to witness the over-incarceration of Black men and women. Right now, the strength of the Black community to call on the spirits, rites, and ways of their ancestors is as crucial as it has ever been.

In addition to being the humble author of this book, and a Voodoo Priestess, I have also been a professional psychic reader for over 35 years. I had someone contact me for a reading the other day, and it was like fate had sent them directly to me. A deep discussion followed as they told me their situation. Very quickly the conversation turned to generational trauma and how to cope with it and, hopefully, transcend its thrall. This woman's life had been plagued with violence, tragedy, and abuse … and yet she'd done her best to show up every day and make a better life. She told me how she had been reading my book *Orishas, Goddesses, and Voodoo Queens* during the past several months of 2020 and how much it had helped her gain perspective about how much beauty and pain is in the history or, more correctly, herstory of BIPOC women. Pioneering author and anthropologist Zora Neale Hurston said that the Black woman is the mule of the Earth. Overworked and overburdened, we frequently need to struggle twice as much for half the payoff. In addition to strength, resilience, and resolve, we also have a long history of magick in our arsenal.

Due to the nature of the BIPOC woman's reality, root magick, Hoodoo, and Conjure are historically less regimented, and the spells and charms crafted here can be created by just about anyone. Very often I get asked about cultural appropriation and the use of the magicks by non-BIPOC. Many of my contemporaries are passionate about this, and, realizing that so much has been stolen over the years, I can't fault them. If people are concerned, I suggest they get a reading. This will open the door to guided access to the traditions. I've seen non-BIPOC turned away from the religion, and I've seen them initiated in it. Getting a reading can answer questions and help provide a much-needed support network.

SPELLS FOR PROTECTION AND PROTEST

Rock Steady Spell

There are many protection spells people can do to prepare themselves, and one is to carry rocks. No, I don't mean for throwing—but crystals for safety and protection. Some good crystals to carry in these protest situations would be clear quartz (for blessings and clarity), black tourmaline (for protection and to transform negativity into positive change), obsidian (for centering and protection), carnelian (for healing and happiness), and turquoise (for success, protection, and longevity). You can perform a simple spell, like rubbing them between your hands, to consecrate these crystals and stones so they will be most effective for you.

Power of Hoodoo Candle Spell

Very often in Hoodoo, some of the prayers come directly from the Bible. In this spell you will gather together all the ingredients and then activate your candle with a passage from scripture. The ingredients you need for this spell are: A seven-day Powerful Hand candle, 3 drops vetivert oil, 3 drops myrrh oil, a small piece of galangal root, 1 cup holy water, glass bowl, white cotton cloth. Place the holy water in the bowl, then add the oils and galangal root. Next, stand over the bowl and recite the following passage from Ephesians 3:20 (King James Bible):

"Now unto him that is able to do exceedingly above all things that we ask or think, according to the power that works in us."

Next, wash your hands in the bowl. Then take the cloth, dip it into the bowl, and use it to wipe down the outside of the candle. Wipe from bottom to top, then top to bottom. Light the candle whenever you need to feel the power of the ancestral universe. (*Note*: Never leave a burning candle unattended.)

Holy Water font, New Orleans. – [photo by author]

•» Fantastic Foremothers Gris-Gris Bag

Queen Nanny, Queen Marie Laveau, and Zora Neale Hurston are just a few of the fantastic foremothers that grace the magickal past of Black women. This gris-gris is designed to be carried with you whenever you wish to connect with its strength. Ingredients: Small purple natural cloth bag, 1 tsp. rosemary herb, 1 tsp. dried hibiscus leaf, 1 tsp. dried violet, 1 tsp. dried rose petals, 1 tsp. graveyard dirt, cotton ball. Place all ingredients into the bag, throw it gently into the air and catch it. This will place it in the hands of the invisibles and then it will be ready to use.

•» Stay Safe Gris-Gris Bag

This gris-gris spell is designed to keep an individual safe. Carry it in your pocket or bag whenever necessary. Ingredients: 1 Tbsp. five-finger grass, 1 Tbsp. dried basil, 1 Tbsp. dried rosemary, 1 Tbsp. caraway seeds, 3 drops myrrh oil, 3 drops vetivert oil, a small Hi John the Conqueror root, a small cloth bag, and a small bowl for mixing. Add all the herbs to the bowl and mix to combine. Then add the drops of vetivert, hyssop, and myrrh oil. Put the mixture in the bag and recite Psalm 51 (KJB) over it:

"Have mercy upon me, O God, according to thy loving kindness: according unto the multitude of thy tender mercies blot out my transgressions.

"Wash me thoroughly from mine iniquity, and cleanse me from my sin.

"For I acknowledge my transgressions: and my sin is ever before me.

"Against thee, thee only, have I sinned, and done this evil in thy sight: that thou mightest be justified when thou speakest, and be clear when thou judgest.

"Behold, I was shapen in iniquity; and in sin did my mother conceive me.

"Behold, thou desirest truth in the inward parts: and in the hidden part thou shalt make me to know wisdom. Purge me with hyssop, and I shall be clean: wash me, and I shall be whiter than snow.

"Make me to hear joy and gladness; that the bones which thou hast broken may rejoice.

"Hide thy face from my sins, and blot out all mine iniquities.

"Create in me a clean heart, O God; and renew a right spirit within me.

"Cast me not away from thy presence; and take not thy holy spirit from me.

"Restore unto me the joy of thy salvation; and uphold me with thy free spirit.

"Then will I teach transgressors thy ways; and sinners shall be converted unto thee.

"Deliver me from bloodguiltiness, O God, thou God of my salvation: and my tongue shall sing aloud of thy righteousness.

" O Lord, open thou my lips; and my mouth shall shew forth thy praise.

"For thou desirest not sacrifice; else would I give it: thou delightest not in burnt offering.

"The sacrifices of God are a broken spirit: a broken and a contrite heart, O God, thou wilt not despise.

"Do good in thy good pleasure unto Zion: build thou the walls of Jerusalem.

"Then shalt thou be pleased with the sacrifices of righteousness, with burnt offering and whole burnt offering: then shall they offer bullocks upon thine altar."

It is now ready to use.

⋅≫ Law Stay Away Powder

It's dangerous to be a Black person in the U.S. and many other parts of the world; frequently, Black people's freedom and their very lives are being threatened. Being hassled by the law for driving or even walking while Black is definitely a thing, and we must do all we can to stay protected. To use this powder, place a small amount in your shoes, your car, or in the corners of your home. Ingredients: 1 Tbsp. cinnamon powder, 1 Tbsp. fennel seed, 1 Tbsp. myrrh powder, 1 Tbsp. clove powder, 1 Tbsp. juniper berries, glass bowl. Combine all ingredients together in the bowl and mix well. Recite the last part of Psalm 142 (KJB) over the mixture.

"Attend unto my cry; for I am brought very low: deliver me from my persecutors; for they are stronger than I. Bring my soul out of prison, that I may praise thy name: the righteous shall compass me about; for thou shalt deal bountifully with me."

Now it is ready to use.

⋅≫ Blessed For Success Bath

This bath is best taken on the full moon but can be used at any time of the month if needs must. If you like, you can make a batch and use it sparingly until you run out. Success depends on skill, knowledge, and also attitude. You must believe you can succeed in order for it to happen. This bath is designed to bring both self-confidence and luck. Ingredients: 9 drops patchouli oil, 9 drops rose oil, 9 drops lavender oil, 9 drops sunflower oil, 9 drops frankincense oil, 2 cups spring water, large glass jar. Add the water to the jar, then add the oils. Close the lid and shake well. Leave the jar on a windowsill for 24 hours so the rays of the moon and the sun will bless it. Shake again. Now it is ready to use. For best results, fill the tub with warm water and add some of the mixture. Get in the tub and visualize success coming toward you in every way you desire. Breathe the scents in deeply and feel the shift in your mind and your soul. Repeat as often as necessary.

⁘⟫ House Blessing Floor Wash for Protection

Recent events have shown that being a BIPOC in the United States means that you might not even be safe in your own home. On March 13, 2020, Breonna Taylor, a 26-years-young Black woman, was killed in her own home by white plainclothes officers in Louisville, Kentucky. It is my sincere hope that all BIPOC protect themselves in every way and never become victims of racism and injustice. This floor wash spell will help to protect your home. A home is supposed to be a place of safety and calm, an oasis against the outside world. This particular formula uses Red Brick Dust. Hoodoo practitioners put Red Brick Dust almost everywhere—the thresholds, the windowsills, the property line … anywhere that needs to be protected. The most effective dust comes from old houses or buildings. It is available online and from many magickal retailers—or, if you are ambitious, you can try to make your own by grinding down an old brick.

With this and all spells in the book, please be sure to get the exact ingredients listed whenever possible. One of my favorite phrases is: In magick, there is no substitute. While our enslaved ancestors may have been forced to make do with available ingredients, part of our experience in the modern age comes from the quest for specific ingredients. Ingredients: 1 Tbsp. Red Brick Dust, 1 Tbsp. black salt, 1 Tbsp. sea salt, 9 drops frankincense oil, 9 drops myrrh oil, 9 drops spearmint oil, 3 drops camphor oil, 1 cup Florida Water, 1 gallon spring water, 1 gallon tap water, wooden spoon (make sure to wash it thoroughly after), and a bucket. Gather all ingredients together, then add the spring water, Florida Water, and the tap water to the bucket. Next add the Red Brick Dust, the black salt, and the sea salt. Stir counterclockwise with the wooden spoon. The next ingredients to go in are the frankincense, myrrh, spearmint, and camphor oils. Again, stir counterclockwise. The mixture is now ready to use. Take a natural fiber cloth and take special care to wipe down the doorsteps, windows, and floors. After this is done, you can wash again with clean water to remove any unsightly residue if you like. Use this wash as often as necessary.

·» Truth and Justice Candle

I almost called this the Lies and Trickerization candle because, in essence, this is what this working is designed to keep you away from. I decided, however, to take the higher road: Focusing on lies will attract lies, while focusing on truth will bring you an atmosphere of truth and honesty. This working requires you to have a space, most likely an altar or table, that you can use temporarily to carry out the burning of this candle. Ingredients: White altar cloth made of a natural material like cotton, candle holder, white plate, 1 Tbsp. dill weed, 1 Tbsp. grains of paradise (or guinea pepper), 1 Tbsp. basil, 1 Tbsp. powdered myrrh, small glass bowl, spoon, small white votive candle, holy water. Spread the cloth out onto your working altar or table. Place the plate in the middle of the table. Put the candle holder in the center of the plate. Add a small amount of holy water to the bottom of the holder. Put the candle in the holder. Take the glass bowl and add the dill weed, grains of paradise, basil, and myrrh. Mix well with the spoon by stirring clockwise until combined. Take this mixture and spread it on the plate around the outside of the candle holder. Light the candle. As it burns, focus on the truth and divine justice coming to you from all different directions. Say whatever words of prayer or concentration you feel coming to you. Prepare for the results, and remember to never leave a burning candle unattended.

·» Ritual to Protect Your Vehicle

Just as I recommend traditional medicine for your body, I recommend traditional maintenance for your car or vehicle. That said, spiritual maintenance on your vehicle is also necessary to help you remain safe and protected while you are traveling in it. Let me begin by saying this spell working is a bit unusual, but it is the most effective one I have found to keep someone safe on the road. Ingredients: A large piece of beef steak (the bloodier the better), ½ ounce iron filings, plastic bag. Take the meat and pour the iron filings over it. Next bring the steak out to your vehicle and rub the four tires of the car with the meat. When you are done, take the meat and put it into the plastic bag. The custom is to dispose of the bag near a railroad tracks, which may be a trash can near the station or crossings, or wherever you see fit. After you leave the bag, turn around and leave without looking back. Repeat this working as often as necessary.

•» Saint Dymphna Candle Working

Saint Dymphna is the patron saint of mental illness and anxiety. She can be a source of inspiration and calm in trying times. Her feast day is celebrated on May 15, and she is given offerings on Mondays (but you can always do this working on another day if needed). Ingredients: Blue candle in glass for Dymphna, 3 drops jasmine oil, 3 drops gardenia oil, 3 drops lemon oil, holy water, small bowl. Place the bowl in the center of your working altar or space. Pour some holy water in the bowl, using just enough to slightly cover the bottom. Add the jasmine, lemon, and gardenia oil to the water. Place the candle in the center of the bowl. Light the candle and say the following prayer:

"Pray for me, St. Dymphna, that I may know peace and courage. That I will not fear, and I will know patience and fortitude."

Repeat whenever necessary.

•» Working to Remove Problem People From Your Space

Everyone has times when there are problematic people standing in the way of your success. This could be an ex-lover, a boss, a neighbor, or just about anyone. I always suggest trying to communicate openly and honestly with someone when you have a problem, but if that doesn't work you may wish to try this working. You will need the person's full legal name and access to a moving body of water, like a river, stream, or ocean. The working is designed to take the person far away from you and stop their difficult behavior from getting to you. Ingredients: Large lemon, paper with the person's name written on it, 9 grains guinea pepper, a silver dime, small white taper candle. Take the lemon and carve out a space large enough to insert your paper and the dime. Place the paper into the hole along with the guinea pepper. Lastly, add the dime. Light the candle and drip the wax on the lemon, covering the hole completely. Next take the lemon to the water. Throw in the lemon, turn around, and don't look back.

Recipes for Revolution

Fortitude Fried Chicken Recipe

In case you missed it, spells can be recipes, too, crafted with magickal ingredients to nourish your body and soul. Onions, garlic, paprika—these are spices of life that make us strong. They were the classic ingredients of our ancestors' fried chicken recipes, and we still love to eat them today. Many of the popular soul food dishes from the southern U.S. grew in popularity because of the necessity of the everyday lives of the enslaved people. Cornbread and fried chicken both traveled well for those seeking their freedom via the Underground Railroad. The Underground Railroad was a complex network of safe houses where runaway enslaved people could find rest on their way to free states or Canada. The foods were chosen for comfort, fortitude, and portability. Over the years it has, unfortunately, evolved into a problematic stereotype. I even have a godchild who is so tired of all these tropes, he refuses to eat chicken in public. I did an event once where the organizer thought it was hilarious to leave a rubber chicken in the Voodoo Woman's bed. However, the past has been cruel enough, Black people have historically been treated horribly, and I say it's high time we had a fried chicken reclaiming. Ingredients: 1 lb. chicken pieces (breasts, legs, whatever you like), ¾ cup flour, 1 tsp. garlic powder, 1 tsp. onion powder, 3 tsp. paprika, ½ tsp. white and ground black pepper, 1 tsp. fresh parsley (minced), pinch of salt, 1 cup buttermilk, grapeseed oil for frying. Clean chicken and pat dry. Place chicken in a bowl and cover with buttermilk. Let sit in the refrigerator for 2 or more hours. Place remaining dry ingredients in a large plastic bowl and mix well. Drain chicken and place into a bag. Shake well to coat. Heat frying oil in a large pan or fryer. When the oil is warm enough to brown a cube of bread quickly, add chicken in a single layer and fry 8-12 minutes on each side. Frying time will depend on size of pieces and temperature of the oil, which should be as close to 350 degrees as possible. Fried chicken is a challenge to cook, and I have seen many a reality cooking show contestant go home trying to make this classic recipe. Make sure the juice of the chicken runs clear when poked with a fork. Remove chicken from pan and drain on brown paper. Eat as soon as possible or freeze for those trips down the road.

•» Protection Beans and Rice

Monday is the traditional day for Red Beans and Rice. These are eaten by New Orleans Voodoo practitioners on Monday for protection. Originally it was cooked on a Monday because this was designated for washing day, and the Creole cooks needed a dish they could put on ahead of time and leave to cook during their busy day. The dish was also a great way to use up some of the leftover Sunday ham, also a Louisiana staple. It is said even Voodoo Queen Marie Laveau had her own version of this dish, and here's one of my favorite recipes. Ingredients: 4 cans red kidney beans (rinsed and drained), 4 cups chicken stock, 2 cups cold water, large yellow onion (chopped), 6 cloves garlic (minced), 3 bay leaves, 3 hot peppers (finely chopped), green pepper (chopped), 2 tsp. apple cider vinegar, 2 tsp. dried thyme, 2 tsp. dried basil, 1/8 cup fresh parsley (diced), 1 Tbsp. fresh rosemary (chopped), 1 lb. pork, cooked and diced (use andouille sausage or ham), 1 tsp. salt, 1 tsp. black pepper, 1 tsp. white pepper, 1 tsp. hot sauce, 3 cups cooked rice. Place beans in a saucepan with water, chicken stock, vinegar, onion, garlic, all the spices, both peppers, hot sauce and pork. Bring to a simmer, stirring frequently. Cook over low heat, continuing to stir for 4-5 hours, making sure it doesn't burn. You may need to add more water if necessary. Remove and discard bay leaves. Adjust salt, pepper, and hot sauce as necessary. Serve over hot cooked rice. Makes 6-8 servings.

·» Bountiful Biscuits

I couldn't complete this section without adding a magickal recipe that includes sweet potatoes. When I was writing my *African American Ritual Cookbook*, I even considered calling it 'A Whole Mess of Things to Make with Sweet Potatoes.' This year I moved into my new house, and the first thing I harvested from the garden was a sweet potato. Both sweet potatoes and yams are said to represent prosperity and harvest in African and Afro-Diasporan culture. The following is my favorite biscuit recipe hands-down. I hope you enjoy it and share the bounty with family and friends. Ingredients: 2 cups flour, 1 tsp. sea salt, 1 Tbsp. baking powder, 1 cup cooked and mashed sweet potato, 1 Tbsp. brown sugar, 1 Tbsp. honey, ½ cup melted butter, ½ tsp. baking soda, ¾ cup sour milk (milk that has literally gone sour). Preheat oven to 400 degrees. Whisk flour, sea salt, and baking powder together in a large bowl. In another bowl mix butter, honey, brown sugar, and sweet potatoes with an electric mixer on low speed. Add baking soda to sour milk, stir, and then let sit. Add sweet potato mixture and milk alternately to the flour mix. Beat well after each addition. Drop biscuits by rounded tablespoon onto an ungreased baking sheet. Bake for 20 minutes or until they start to turn golden brown on top and a toothpick inserted into the center comes out clean. Serve warm with butter and/or honey. Makes about a dozen biscuits.

·» Lucky Greens

If you talk about food and Black culture in the United States, the conversation very quickly turns to greens. Greens are eaten on New Year's Day and throughout the year to bring money, luck, and prosperity. Undoubtedly, there are as many recipes for greens as there are people. The most important thing to remember is to rip the greens apart with your bare hands—cutting them will spoil the magick. Ingredients: 6 cups washed and torn greens (collards, mustard, or other), 3 slices bacon, 2 cloves garlic (minced), 1 yellow onion (chopped), 1 cup chicken broth, ½ cup coconut milk, 1 Tbsp. olive oil, salt and pepper to taste. Place bacon in the bottom of a saucepan. Cook over low heat for 2 minutes, then add onion and cook until it begins to brown. Next add the garlic and continue cooking until bacon gets crispy. Remove bacon and cool. Add olive oil and greens, then cook for 1 minute. Add chicken broth and cook over low heat, stirring occasionally. After 30 minutes or when the greens begin to fully break down, crumble the bacon and add it back to the pan along with the coconut milk. Cook for another 30 minutes, stirring frequently. Serves 4-6.

•» Healing Rice

Rice is an ingredient used in many cuisines of the world to bring healing and abundance. Here's a simple rice recipe to bring healing to your community, family, and yourself. Ingredients: 1 cup water, 1 cup coconut water, 1 Tbsp. butter, 1 tsp. dried basil, 1 tsp. dried parsley, 1 tsp. dried thyme, 1 cup white rice. Place all ingredients except the rice in a saucepan over medium heat and bring to a simmer. When it begins to bubble, turn the heat down to low, add the rice, and cover. Cook for 20 minutes or until rice is tender and the water is all absorbed. Serves 2-4.

NIA AND UMOJA
PURPOSE AND UNITY IN THE COMMUNITY

Interest surrounding the African Traditional Religions has grown exponentially in recent years. Voodoo, Hoodoo, Vodou, and the like went from being secretive and misunderstood to being loud and proud. For hundreds of years these were kept secret because, in part, this was necessary to keep the practitioners safe and secure. This strengthened the community in many ways but also allowed some negative practices, occasionally even criminal ones, to continue undiscovered. A religion is never defined by a single individual but by the collective behavior of its followers.

Unity in these traditions is bound by respect. Respect is to be shown to honored elders in the tradition, which helps to reinforce the sacred circle of life. By no means is that to imply that there aren't negative people in the community, but this is true of almost any organization. Those aberrations should be dealt with accordingly but shouldn't be used as a reason to abandon the concept of a spiritual family. People like to drag these traditions down to the lowest common denominator. If I had a dollar for every time someone tried to capitalize on a Voodoo crime, I would be a rich person. Kwanzaa is a cultural holiday created by and for Black people to celebrate their cultural heritage. The first principle of the holiday is called Umoja, which in the Swahili language means "unity." It is most likely derived from the all-female Umoja village in Umoja, Kenya. Founded on the basis of women's rights, this village started out as a refuge for survivors of abuse. Here, they created a family and support network. Spiritual organizations in the ATRs are also seen as chosen family and designed to provide a complex support network. I'm the first person to realize that, like all families, these can be tricky to navigate effectively, but we must put in the work in all areas to make sure these connections are kept alive.

In all of these traditions, people come together for feasts, initiations, celebrations, and divination. Every one of these instances provides an opportunity for strengthening oneself and one's community, and it doesn't stop there. Many spiritual houses also offer support to their local communities by fundraising and providing food, support, and other services. My own group, The House of Maman Brigitte, has been donating to food drives and collecting dolls for The Black Doll Project (which provides dolls for BIPOC children that look like them) since it began. Their website says, "In 2017 we initiated the Black Doll Project as an act of affirmation by sending Black Dolls to the Caribbean to assert the love and power of our Blackness, our Negritude. As people of color we have been stigmatized by the lack of representation in media outlets. What has infused our collective narratives is the perception that we are less than, non-existent, and our worth has been devalued. By sending a Black Doll to a child in the Caribbean we are reaffirming our existence and empowering our children to love, see and imagine their future selves. Our message is a reminder that they are valued and that they matter. Please consider donating a doll today." This is just one way you can give back to the wider BIPOC community and raise up those in need. I'm sure there are several nonprofit organizations in your local area to which you can donate. We are most empowered when we seek to empower others.

Actions like this help to support our purpose, which is ultimately to make things better for ourselves and other BIPOC through magick, fundraising, education, and whatever means necessary. If we look back at Kwanzaa, one of the principles is called Nia, which is the Swahili word for "purpose." In many ways, the African Traditional Religions focus their purpose onto the individual and the community being aligned with their proper path. That path is not always easy, but it is necessary. I see so much jealousy and contempt among Black people, most days it hurts my heart. There are still rays of hope, however, when I see the community uplift each other, because we are most certainly stronger together.

We must sing it loud that Black lives matter now and always. Here's a poem I wrote in sympathy for all the mothers and the babies.

Big and Little Black Lives Matter

This is some writing that's fueled by tears
Born in deep pain, and fed on real fears.
Most days it's sad thoughts, not words that appear—
For people taken too soon, people who still should be here.

These thoughts are from a mother whose child is gone
I understand these women whose purpose has passed on.
I applaud those with the strength yell loud,
The closest they can get to their babies is to reach at a cloud.

PLANT ROOTS, HARVEST FOOD

The spells, stories, and suggestions contained in this chapter are designed to help plant seeds of empowerment and success against a multitude of odds. It is my hope that, through these words and actions, you will be able to harvest all the bounty and joy you deserve. It is worth saying, however, that divination will help you to navigate your way through life and help you choose which spells or workings may be best for you to focus on in the present. I urge everyone to rely on their spiritual teachers for guidance and psychic readings and, whenever possible, rely on yourself, too. Initiates of La Regla Lucumí are encouraged to do a reading by throwing cocos or performing other types of divination when they are confronted with difficult situations or choices. For day-to-day challenges, I often suggest people outside of a formalized spiritual house cultivate a good yes-or-no system of divination that they can perform on their own. This could be reading cards, tarot, or using a pendulum or dowsing rods. If you are beginner with these systems, my best advice is to test and verify the results you are getting. Start by asking simple questions like, "Is it going to rain on me today, or will I get a letter in the mail?" Once you get comfortable with your divination tools, you can start to ask more relevant questions. For big decisions, I still recommend consulting with a seasoned professional.

With guidance and care, we can all hope to guide our lives toward the best possible destiny. We can draw on the strength and power of our ancestors to create a new and better future.

CHAPTER TWELVE
VOODOO GOLD AT THE RAINBOW'S END

In recent times, there has been a gradual evolution of attitudes toward Voodoo and Santería. In my many years of both private and public practice, I have unfortunately seen racism, ignorance, disrespect, paranoia, and curiosity. In the beginning, I was constantly amazed that followers of religions such as Christianity, Judaism, Witchcraft and others that have such a tragic and vast history of persecution could turn right around and be so intolerant themselves.

The reason for this intolerance is partly ignorance. The media's characterization of Voodoo and Santería has been to portray them as evil, perverse, and diabolical. Throughout history those in power have falsely accused those that they feared of the most atrocious crimes. It happened in ancient times and, unfortunately, it still occurs today.

By lecturing at universities and events, and by publishing respectful and accurate information about the Afro-Diasporic religious traditions, I have attempted to counteract some of these extremely negative stereotypes. There is, however, still quite a way to go. Within the La Regla Lucumí and Voodoo community, it is not uncommon to hear about people having trouble with the authorities because of their beliefs. Legally, these range from troubles about sacrifice, to public drumming, to child custody.

Forty years ago, many public events had a prohibition against drumming. Drumming is an integral part of these religions. It is through the drums that the Lwa and Orisha are honored and called. Percussive sound and worship are inseparable. Thankfully, over the years, this taboo has been lifted, yet tension still remains. Again, I hope knowledge and training will help to remove some of the residual tension. Voodoo and Santería rhythms are both specific and complex. Those wishing to play with these drummers should take the time to familiarize themselves with the rhythms. This can be done by finding a teacher or studying the recordings suggested in this book.

A lot of the prejudice against Voodoo, I believe, stems from misconceptions about possession and sacrifice, which I have touched on throughout this book. People are terrified of losing control—they fear that somehow they will attend a ceremony and lose themselves. Possession is not that type of experience; I have never heard of anyone becoming possessed and not returning to his or her normal self afterward. I also frequently hear stereotypical beliefs concerning animal sacrifice. As if the world is populated by vegans, they seem to believe that Voodoo practitioners are barbaric primitives. They condemned the behavior, I believe, because they doubt its success. Most would not think twice about using an animal medicine to treat a terminal illness, but when Lucumí and Voodoo temples reach for a similar solution to a serious problem, they are vilified. Animal sacrifice is done to alleviate serious problems within the community. When an animal is sacrificed, the practitioner enters into a battle of wills with it. The practitioner believes that only one being will emerge victorious, and he or she knows that he or she may not come out alive. In fact, Voodoo and Santería priests and priestesses are notorious for dying under mysterious circumstances during a ritual. This is accepted within the community as a mere fact of life. Sacrifice can come in many forms.

This generally antagonistic public attitude toward Voodoo and the other African Diasporic Religions is steadily changing, along with some of the other prejudices. Now, when I host a large public ritual, there are fewer threats and disruptions from the community. That doesn't mean things have shifted much in the public mind or in the popular media. I still want to start a Voodoo Anti-Defamation League every time I see an offensive film like Voodoo Dawn or some other pulp horror movie. Unfortunately, the veil of secrecy that has been in place to protect the religion from persecution has also allowed outsiders to retain their ignorance. Somehow, I believe that if more people knew that their local postal carrier or neighborly college professor was an ATR practitioner, they might be less likely to jump to the wrong conclusions.

Hopefully, the public image will change, although I do have to admit that someone said to me the other day, "You're OK. At least you don't practice Santería"—which I obviously do! Voodoo and Lucumí practices need not remain completely clandestine or they will forever be the scapegoat for people's misguided imagination. Indeed, the risk of persecution may increase, but eventually so will people's tolerance.

Someday, maybe children will learn the myths and legends of Changó and Oyá in school the way they do those of Isis and Zeus. Maybe someday, when I write 'Voodoo' in as a religion on a hospital questionnaire, the administrator won't ask, "Do you really want me to put that down?" Television commercials will someday stop referring to Voodoo in terms of dolls, pins, and primitive practices. Hopefully, the words "freedom of religion" will eventually mean "freedom of religion in the United States." Perhaps West African religious holidays will be celebrated and respected just like more mainstream religions. Vendors will sell palm fronds on the street for Ayizan's feast day, and not just for Palm Sunday. One day, the United States will have its own African Diasporic spiritual registry, similar to what is in place in Brazil, so people can investigate the lineage and practices of a prospective spiritual teacher. Vévé tattoos will become as popular as those with Asian characters. Maybe someday Black rap stars will sing, "Orisha walk with me," in praise of the ancient gods. Voodoo is a serious religion and, hopefully, it will be treated as such by the general public.

Some things are changing for the better, however slowly uphill the journey may be. The past 35 years have seen the rediscovery of priceless Voodoo information gathered by the African American anthropology pioneer and priestess Zora Neale Hurston; the advent of the internet, which allows practitioners to find and stay connected to each other across vast distances; and the publication of a wealth of information about Santería, Palo Mayombe, Candomblé, Vodou, and other African-derived traditions. Hopefully, more wonderful surprises like these will continue to occur, adding to the religions in ways we didn't even imagine were possible.

It has been well over a decade since I originally wrote much of what is written above. While I have seen the popularity of the traditions grow over the years, there is still prejudice, cultural appropriation, and racism plaguing us on every level. Many new practitioners have failed to see the beauty and power in these ancient systems and, in some cases, are trying to buck the system. Phrases like "intuitive magick" and "unverified personal gnosis" have entered into the religion and, without calling anyone out specifically, I think many of these practitioners are missing the bigger picture. I'm not trying to "yuck anyone's yum," as my younger friends say, but learning the ways of our foremothers and forefathers in the tradition will help to improve our magick and our lives.

I have also seen some good unfold over the years. In many ways, the African Traditional Religions have come out of the basement, the closet, and everywhere else they were forced to hide. I've seen Riva Nyri Precil's Fete Gede ceremony, which I attended, covered in the New York Times. I have seen and held open conversations and workshops about the traditions. My blog, Voodoo Universe, has even grown to be the top ATR blog in the world with over 150,000 views a year. Now when I tell a hospital administrator or cab driver I practice Voodoo, no one bats an eyelash—of course I live in New Orleans now, so that helps a lot. These things make my heart smile. The splendor and glory of these ways are finally coming to light.

Marie Laveau altar photo for St. John's Eve. – [photo by author]

Ago Ago Ye-Orisha Please Hear Us!

APPENDIX ONE
RECOMMENDED READING AND RECORDINGS

YORUBA AND AFRICAN IFÁ

Abimbola, Wande. *Yoruba Divination Poetry*. London: Nok Publishers, 1977. I highly recommend this book or any of the others by Abimbola. A university professor in Boston, this man is a wealth of information on Yoruba thought and religion.

Akintola, Akinbowale. *Yoruba Ethics and Metaphysics: Being Basic Philosophy Underlying the Ifa System of Thought of the Yoruba*. Ogbomoso, Nigeria: Valour Publishing Ventures, 1999. This is the kind of book I love to see, a manuscript on Yoruba cosmology and thought by a Nigerian professor. The work details the Ifá system of thought (like the title says) in an artful and comprehensive way using mythology, history, and the Odus (divination story/proverb lessons).

Barnes, Sandra T. *Ogun: An Old God for a New Age*. Philadelphia: Institute for the Study of Human Issues, 1980. Barnes does a wonderful job of explaining and presenting theories about sacred iron and this formidable Orisha.

Courlander, Harold. *Tales of Yoruba Gods and Heroes*. New York: Crown Publishers, 1973. Written dozens of years ago, this book focuses on classical Yoruba mythology.

Fatunmbi, Awo FaLokun. ***Iwa-pele Ifa Quest: The Search for the Source of Santería and Lucumi***. New York: Original Publications, 1991. Fatunmbi in this work, as well as in his Orisha series, provides an overview of the modern practices and systems of thought in the religion. This is recommended as a good jumping-off point for beginners.

Galembo, Phyllis. ***Divine Inspiration: From Benin to Bahia***. Albuquerque: University of New Mexico Press, 1993. See the description under the chapter on Candomblé and Brazilian tradition.

Idowu, E. Bolaji. ***Olódúmaré: God in Yoruba Belief***. New York: Original Publications, 1995. This is another book focusing on a single Orisha and the accompanying worship and mythology. It provides a fantastic amount of detailed information about this creator deity for anyone who wishes to learn more.

Mason, John. ***Orisa Black Gods New World***. New York: Yoruba Theological Archministry, 2016. Baba John Mason has been a leader in the community since the early 1970s. I've had the pleasure of meeting him on a few occasions, and he provides a great wisdom and clarity in all of his work.

Matory, J. Lorand. ***Sex and the Empire That Is No More: Gender and the Politics of Metaphor in Oyo Yoruba Religion***. Minneapolis: University of Minnesota Press, 1994. A comprehensive look at gender roles and transitions among the Oyo people.

McKenzie, Peter. ***Hail Orisha! A Phenomenology of a West African Religion in the Mid-nineteenth Century***. New York: Brill, 1997. This long-overdue work details the written accounts of Orisha tradition in the 1800s and is valuable for any serious historian.

Olupona, Jacob K., ed. ***African Traditional Religions in Contemporary Society***. New York: Paragon House, 1991. This great collection contains essays from such notable scholars as Wande Abimbola and John

S. Mbiti. It explores such diverse topics as the talking drum and the role of women. The book is certainly worth taking a look at.

Soyinka, Wole. ***Myth, Literature, and the African World.*** Cambridge, UK: Cambridge University Press, 1976. Soyinka is an entertaining writer who incorporates variations occurring in Afro-Atlantic traditions. This is a useful and informative work.

Thompson, Robert Farris. ***Flash of the Spirit: African and Afro-American Art and Philosophy.*** New York: Random House, 1983. This book by Thompson, a Yale professor of African and African American art, gives a comprehensive examination of ritual art and its related religious practices. Always scholarly without sacrificing the aesthetic beauty of the items, this book is highly recommended, along with his other work, Face of the Gods: Art and Altars of Africa and the African Americas. New York: Museum for African Art, 1993.

VODOU

Brown, Karen McCarthy. ***Mama Lola.*** Berkeley: University of California Press, 1991. An interesting account of a Vodou priestess in Brooklyn, my hometown. Brown was an anthropologist and an initiate who provided an exciting look at how the traditional Haitian practices are renegotiated in the Diaspora.

Cosentino, Donald J., ed. ***The Sacred Arts of Haitian Vodou.*** Los Angeles: Fowler Museum, 1995. This is the accompanying book for the museum exhibit created by Cosentino. It is a visual treasure with photographs of many Haitian ritual items.

Consentino, Donald J. ***Vodou Things: The Art of Pierrot Barra and Marie Cassaise.*** Jackson: University Press of Mississippi, 1998. The artists covered here push the boundaries of what is known as "outsider art." They recycle items from Port-au-Prince's Iron Market, such as scrap metal, old tools, and toys, and combine them with elements of Haitian flag-making, such as sequins, beads, and Catholic imagery.

Crosley, Reginald. *The Vodou Quantum Leap: Alternative Realities, Power, and Mysticism*. St. Paul, MN: Llewellyn, 2000. Crosley has written a scholarly book that traverses theories such as relativity and chaos. The book delves into the alternate reality of Afro-Haitian culture. The book will not only help readers to understand subjects such as possession and adorcism, black magick, and transcendence, but may also guide them to their own creative thinking in these areas.

Demangles, Leslie. *Faces of the Gods*. Durham: University of North Carolina Press, 1992. This book provides an in-depth look at the Lwa and the practices of Voodoo.

Deren, Maya. *Divine Horseman: The Living Gods of Haiti*. New York: Thames and Hudson, 1953. It is impossible to do justice to Deren in the limited space allotted here. There have been multivolume books published about her exotic life, visionary art, and theories. Her theories deal with time and movement and how they function for an audience and performer. This book beautifully contains the ethnographic data she collected on her trip to Haiti. She also shot several hours of film during the trip that was later edited down and released posthumously by her husband.

Dunham, Katherine. *Island Possessed and Dances of Haiti*. Garden City, NY: Doubleday, 1969 and 1938, respectively. Dunham is a powerful African American pioneer in dance, anthropology, and even Hollywood. I highly recommend all her work and hope that she will finally achieve her rightful place as a living legend of cultural advancement.

Gordon, Leah. *The Book of Vodou: Charms and Rituals to Empower Your Life*. Hauppauge, NY: Barron's Educational Series, 2000. This beautifully illustrated book provides basic information about the religion. A few basic spells are included, but this book is really best used for the elaborate photographs of ritual items.

Hurbon, Laennec. ***Voodoo: Search for the Spirit***. New York: Abrams, 1995. This is a fantastic book, one that I recommend to almost anyone wishing to look at the history and religious tradition of Haitian Vodou. It features amazing photos of flags and rituals.

Hurston, Zora Neale. ***Tell My Horse***. Berkeley, CA: Turtle Island Foundation, 1981. Hurston was a pioneer anthropologist, ethnographic filmmaker, folklorist, Vodou practitioner, and author. This book details the practices of Vodou in Haiti and Jamaica that she collected during her ethnographic research conducted during the 1930s. It is an eloquent and practical resource for anyone wishing to explore the history of the tradition. An ad in the New York Times Book Review from 1938 quotes early Vodou scholar William Seabrook, "Papa Legba opened wide the gate for her—and Zora has come through as no white ever could."

MacAllister, Elizabeth. ***Vodou in New York***. PhD diss. Yale University, 1990. This book displays a bit of everything: history, practice, economic and political considerations, art, music, and the Caribbean "resistance movement" in the religion as practiced in New York City.

Rigaud, Milo. ***Vévé*** and ***Secrets of Voodoo***. New York: Pocket Books, 1971. Rigaud, an anthropologist and native of Haiti, conducted extensive research into the religion of Voodoo from the 1930s onward. The vévé book has the most extensive sampling of the symbols to be found in print. He includes several vévés for Legba, Erzulie, Ogou, Gran Bois, ShiLiBo, and others.

Wilcken, Lois. ***The Drums of Voodoo***. Tempe, AZ: White Cliffs Media, 1992. This book explores one of the more popular elements of Haitian Vodou tradition: sacred drumming. An overview of the various practices is given and serves as a springboard for the beginning drummer.

NEW ORLEANS VOODOO AND HOODOO

Dorsey, Lilith. ***Orishas, Goddesses, and Voodoo Queens.*** Weiser, 2020. This is my most recent book focusing on the divine feminine in the form of the Lwas, Orishas, and most specifically the Voodoo Queens. It is full of history, herstory, spells, and wisdom relating not only to New Orleans Voodoo but all the African Traditional Religions.

Gandolfo, Charles. ***Voodoo Vévés and Talismans.*** New Orleans: New Orleans Historic Voodoo Museum, publication date unknown. Written by the former curator of the New Orleans Voodoo Museum, this is a brief guide to various vévé images used in the New Orleans area. It also provides some instruction for using the vévé images as magickal talismans to carry with you. The book is available from the museum.

Glassman, Sallie Ann. ***Vodou Visions: An Encounter with Divine Mystery.*** New York: Villard, 2000. Glassman is a powerful and successful priestess with her own spiritual house in New Orleans. An initiated mambo, she practices both New Orleans Voodoo and Haitian Vodou. Her take on the Lwa and Orisha is a unique one and well worth reading.

Haskins, Jim. ***Voodoo and Hoodoo.*** Bronx, NY: Original Publications, 1978. This book provides a bit of New Orleans historical lore alongside a plethora of information on various spellcraft. Just be careful what you wish for.

Malbrough, Ray T. ***Magical Power of the Saints.*** St. Paul, MN: Llewellyn, 2000. A valuable guide to the various images and offerings for the different saints. The only problem I have is that I wish Malbrough included more of this wonderful information.

Martinié, Louis. ***Waters of Return: The Aeonic Flow of Voodoo.*** New Orleans, LA: Black Moon Publishing, 1986. Martinié explores the ritual and symbolism of one of his favorite topics: the Marassa, or divine twins. This chapbook is both informative and transformational in its eloquence. It is definitely worth purchasing, and all proceeds are donated for the relief of the poor.

Martinié, Louis, and Sallie Ann Glassman. ***The New Orleans Voodoo Tarot.*** Rochester, VT: Inner Traditions, 1992. This is an amazing book and visually intriguing deck. Martinié and Glassman are wonderful and powerful people. I strongly recommend this work. It provides information on many different levels to appeal to everyone from the beginner to the most serious practitioner. This was the first African American Tarot deck and is, in my opinion, the one of the best available, bridging the gaps between Voodoo, Tarot, and Kabbalah.

Reed, Ishmael. ***Mumbo Jumbo.*** New York: Macmillan, 1972. Reed does for Voodoo and Hoodoo what Jorge Amado does for Candomblé: He takes a mystical and entertaining subject and produces a surrealistic novel revolving around African Diasporic Religion. If you enjoy this, please be sure to look at his poetry.

Sen Elias, ***Crescent City Conjure Comprehensive Guide.*** Here you will find information about common Hoodoo terms, candles, oils, gris-gris ("a little spirit companion that has the ability to assist in a desired goal"), spiritual baths, spiritual soaps, and conjure powders. There is even a segment dedicated to curious curios. Here are all the conjure creations our foremamas knew, even if they didn't speak about them often. There are crossed coffin nails, chicken foot charms, and railroad spikes.

Teish, Luisah. ***Jambalaya.*** San Francisco, CA: Harper and Row, 1985. Teish is a Louisiana native and Yoruba priestess, poetess, and author. As a daughter of Oshún, her work is refreshing and a good place to start for those coming from other spiritual traditions. This book has been the gold standard in the traditions since it was published, and it is a must for every practitioner's library.

TRINIDAD

Henry, Frances. *Reclaiming African Religions in Trinidad: The Socio-political Legitimation of the Orisha and Spiritual Baptist Faiths*. Trinidad and Tobago: University of the West Indies Press, 2003. This is a typical ethnography describing the practices of the people of Trinidad, both historically and in the context of the present day.

Houk, James T. *Spirits, Blood, and Drums: The Orisha Religion in Trinidad*. Philadelphia, PA: Temple University Press, 1995. Houk surveys the religion and discusses the practices that he witnessed firsthand. A bit dry at times, this is still an important text, considering the lack of information on the subject.

Lum, Kenneth Anthony. *Praising His Name in the Dance: Spirit Possession in the Spiritual Baptist Faith and Orisha Work in Trinidad, West Indies*. Singapore: Harwood Academic, 2000. This ethnography explores cosmology, history, and comparisons.

SANTERÍA OR LA REGLA LUCUMÍ

Barnett, Miguel. *Afro-Cuban Religions*. Princeton, NJ: Markus Weiner Publishers, 2001. A simple description of the range of practices occurring in Cuba. It features a section on Palo Monte that, like much of the writings on the tradition, focuses on the negative potential of the practices to do evil, rather than on the positive magick that I have found to be in place for healing and contact with the dead. The book does feature an interesting array of firmas (ritual line drawings) for the deities, visually similar to Haitian vévés, as well as other exciting photos and drawings.

Cabrera, Lydia. *Yemaya Y Ochún and El Monte*. Miami: Edi- cones Universal, 1980 and 1975, respectively. These are classic Spanish texts relating to the tradition.

De La Torre, Miguel A. *Santería: The Beliefs and Rituals of a Growing Religion in America*. Grand Rapids, MI: William B. Eerdmans, 2004. This book does what I have been waiting for. It presents Santería from a respectful, scholarly standpoint while addressing the truth and validity of the religion. De La Torre includes detailed information about Santería initiations and divination, including the Chinese dream and lottery number correspondence list.

Flores-Pena, Ysamur, and Roberta J. Evanchuk. *Santería Garments and Altars*. Jackson: University of Mississippi Press, 1994. A beautiful and informative book that gives a look at the ritual garments and altars of the religion. The creations are all inspirational and divine.

Gleason, Judith. *Oyá: In Praise of the Goddess*. Boston: Shambala, 1987. An in-depth look at this wonderful Orisha of change, cemeteries, and the tornado. It does, however, get a bit scholarly at times.

Montenegro, Carlos. *Santería: Candles, Herbs, Incense, and Oils*. Plainview, NY: Original Publications, 1994. A must-have for practitioners in the tradition. Montenegro provides a wealth of herbal information. Formerly titled *Santería Formulary*, this book provides herbal formulas for just about every situation, including fertility, victory, gambling, and more. I would also recommend Montenegro's book *Powerful Amulets of Santería*. I had a chance to interview Montenegro years ago and found him to be charming, knowledgeable, and powerful.

Murphy, Joseph M. *Santería: African Spirits in Latin America*. Boston: Beacon Press, 1988. A brief history and overview of the religion. Enhanced by several of the author's personal accounts of his research among Santería communities in the Bronx.

Núñez, Luis Manuel. *Santería: A Practical Guide to Afro-Caribbean Magic*. Dallas, TX: Spring Publications, 1992. An entertaining and knowledgeable man, Núñez offers a comprehensive look at the tradition, provides detailed lists of offerings, and tells the most popular stories of the Orisha. Núñez was a member of the Voodoo Spiritual Temple in its early years. He has since passed, but he is truly missed.

Perez, Elizabeth. *Religion in the Kitchen*. NYU Press, 2016. Taste your honey, thank your ancestors, Elizabeth Perez's book Religion in the Kitchen reminds us of the important rituals and rites surrounding food in the African Traditional Religions. Food is such a large part of the traditions, and anyone interested in exploring why should check out this fantastic work.

Santiago, Miguel F. *Dancing with the Saints*. Puerto Rico: Inter-American University Press, 1993. A journalist's brief look at the religion.

Vega, Marta Moreno. *The Altar of My Soul: The Living Traditions of Santería*. Like myself, Vega is a professor, a practitioner, and a New Yorker. She details various aspects of the tradition while giving us valuable insight into her own journey. It is a very valuable work.

AFRO-BRAZILIAN

Amado, Jorge. *Tent of Miracles*. Madison: University of Wisconsin Press, 2003. All of Amado's work is brilliant prose that reads like magickal poetry. A Candomblé adept himself, Amado really makes the world of the Orixa come alive. His novels are peppered with Orixa recipes and herbal preparations and are always an exhilaratingly good read.

Brown, Diana DeG. *Umbanda: Religion and Politics in Urban Brazil*. Ann Arbor, MI: UMI Research Press, 1986. Brown writes a phenomenal ethnographic account of the history, practices, and sociocultural context of the religion of Umbanda.

Galembo, Phyllis. *Divine Inspiration: From Benin to Bahia*. Albuquerque: University of New Mexico Press, 1993. This book contains beautiful photographs and informative essays. Of particular note is an essay by the eloquent and charming Zeca Ligiéro. He artfully gives a brief overview of the tradition and even mentions Carmen Miranda. I had the chance to hear Ligiéro speak a few years back, and I highly recommend his work.

Harding, Rachel E.: *A Refuge in Thunder: Candomblé and Alternative Spaces of Blackness*. Bloomington: Indiana University Press, 2000.

Langguth, A. J. *Macumba: White and Black Magic in Brazil*. New York: Harper and Row, 1975. Like many manuscripts of the time, this details one person's account into the mysterious world of Macumba. A bit long on exposition and short on scholarly research, this story does, however, make an interesting read as one of the earliest English-language works about the subject.

Voeks, Robert A. *Sacred Leaves of Candomblé: African Magic, Medicine, and Religion in Brazil*. Austin: University of Texas Press, 1997. Voeks takes on the necessary and difficult job of classifying the numerous plants and herbal medicines utilized in the religion of Candomblé. He also provides a brief description of the herbal practices and rituals of the religion. Somehow, he does all this in an exciting and enjoyable way.

Wafer, Jim. *Taste of Blood: Spirit Possession in Brazilian Candomblé*. Philadelphia: University of Pennsylvania Press, 1991. This book examines the basics of the religion. A bit scholarly at times, as it delves into the theories of Bakhtin, it is overall very comprehensive and informative.

AFRICAN TRADITIONAL RELIGIOUS MUSIC

Action of Grace and The Drum and the Chalice by Rev. Bonnie Devlin. A phenomenal CD by Gros Mambo Bonnie Devlin. I have studied with and performed ritual beside Devlin and, although she recently passed, she will always be very dear to my heart. She designed these CDs to be a complete musical accompaniment for a private Vodou ritual. Devlin does all the ritual calls and chants for the Lwa in Creole and then plays the different parts of the polyrhythmic beats.

Drums of Passion: The Beat by Babatunde Olatunji. Ryvsc, 1989. This amazing CD, produced by the drummer and pioneer ethnomusicological archivist Mickey Hart, features the most famous African drummer of the modern era: Babatunde Olatunji. This explores some of the sacred words and chants of Yoruba religion and is sure to please.

Festival and Ritual Drumming by Louis Martinié. An audio tape of a series of ritual drum sessions by this master drummer, author, and priest.

Perle De Culture by Riva Nyri Precil. This collection features music for Danbala, Papa Legba, and Loko. Precil is an amazing musician, poet, and author. Her work is powerful and transformational—please add it to your collection.

Tribal Magik by Dragon Ritual Drummers. This is just one of the phenomenal CDs that are put out by Witchdoctor Utu and the Dragon Ritual Drummers. Utu has been a fixture at the Voodoo Spiritual Temple and is my spiritual brother and friend for over 20 years. I highly recommend all their work.

Voodoo by Priestess Miriam Chamani and Louis Martinie, with Jim YaYa, Luis Núñez, Chris Li, Joey LaCaze, Papa Gran Bwa Bakavi, and Don Dufrane. This great CD from the Voodoo Spiritual Temple includes songs for Legba, Changó, Mama Waters, Gede, Ogun, and the Yanvalou, to name a few. It is available from the Voodoo Spiritual Temple or online at voodoospiritualtemple.org

APPENDIX TWO
RESOURCES FOR AFRICAN TRADITIONAL RELIGION

For better or worse, the Information Age has opened up a vast range of possibilities to obtain knowledge. When I started my newsletter, Oshún-African Magickal Quarterly, and its accompanying website, Branwen's Pantry, in the early part of 1996, there were few, if any, facts about African Traditional Religions on the internet. These publications offered information, products, and services to people across the globe. I believe that access to this knowledge can do a lot to dispel the multitude of myths and misconceptions about these religions. Zombies, evil dolls with pins, and demonic possession have no place in the serious practice of the religions. While secrets do surround the traditions of Voodoo and Lucumí, I certainly do not advocate all these secrets and ceremonial mysteries that are being instantly exposed.

Lucumí, Voodoo, Candomblé, Ifá, and all the other African Religious Traditions I have been discussing, function at their core in a parent-child type of bond. This bond cannot be made through a machine like the computer. What the internet is great for in this context is both providing basic information to the public and improving communication between members of the community. For hundreds of years, the public conception of religions like New Orleans Voodoo and the rest has been that they are evil, focused on revenge, pins, and blood. Access to accurate information provides the thinking public with a way to eradicate these negative stereotypes and get a glimpse at the real truth for themselves. The online world is believed by many to be the domain of the Orisha Ogún, who also rules medicine and war. In this aspect of Ogún, communication across distant lands is highlighted.

The advent of computer technology has allowed the improvement of communication between spiritual houses and families. Practitioners are now able to communicate across vast distances, and I frequently hear stories about how people have rediscovered long-lost spiritual family members online. In African Traditional Religions, a strong emphasis is placed on one's sacred lineage: With modern technology, people are better afforded the chance to explore their own global and local lineages. In addition to providing increased access to individuals, the internet allows practitioners to obtain hard-to-find spiritual ingredients and written materials.

Not everything about going online has been beneficial to furthering African Diasporic religious traditions, however. A proliferation of websites has also extremely increased the number of con artists attempting to falsely profit from the religion. One of the biggest traps of the Information Age is that not all knowledge can be considered equally valid. Please check all your online information with both your spiritual teachers and accredited academic sources.

There are numerous places online to purchase sacred items. I would like to say: Please be cautious, especially with auction sites. The listings sometimes remind me of the people who used to sell splinters from The Cross. A lot of times, what they are selling as a recently discovered super holy piece of crap is just that. If it sounds too good to be true and it costs 99 cents, you should probably look elsewhere. Now, there are stories where people are able to obtain rare and sacred items once all the parties are able to verify with whom they are dealing. I would also like to mention that, unfortunately, many of the commercially available bulk supplies are of substandard quality. One Santero even told me a major company substitutes ingredients of traditional formulas so it can use up the surplus herbs and oils it has. The best way to think of it is as the difference between buying a suit off the rack and having one made for your body. There are several *botanicas* (Lucumí spiritual supply stores) in larger cities and online that carry both premade preparations and custom-blended items. Several also offer divination services and other necessary items, such as herbs and candles. My only advice for going to a botanica in person is to remain composed and respectful at all times and, if possible, bring a native Spanish speaker. Going to a botanica is almost always a quest. I remember going once to purchase supplies for a Changó feast and the building across the street was on fire. Everyone was fine, but it did seem oddly epic.

The following is a partial overview of some of the African Traditional Religious sites and botanicas out there:

Black Moon Publishing
www.blackmoonpublishing.com

This is one of the best sites out there providing a wealth of information about New Orleans Voodoo and other magickal traditions. It has a great archive of magickal records, including my piece titled, "Dr. John Montanee: The Physician's Message is Know Thyself."

Voodoo Spiritual Temple
1428 N Rampart St., New Orleans, LA 70116

(504) 943-9795

www.voodoospiritualtemple.org

Run by Priestess Miriam Chamani, this is a fantastic website for her physical temple and shop in New Orleans, which offers a variety of spiritual and magickal items, services, and much wisdom from the temple. "Cycles come and cycles go, only to be repeated again."

Voodoo Universe Blog
www.patheos.com/blogs/voodoouniverse

I began the Voodoo Universe blog in 2014 to provide accurate and respectful information about all the ATRs. Little did I know it would grow to be the most popular Voodoo blog in the world, with over 150,000 hits a year and over 650 posts. Invariably when someone has a question, I ask them to check the blog first. Voodoo Universe is a wealth of information about practices, Orisha, Lwa, workings, spells, recipes, and a hell of a lot more.

OrishaNet
orishanet.org

OrishaNet is one of the oldest Lucumí, or traditional Santería, sites on the internet. The mission statement says, "OrishaNet is dedicated to being the premier source of information about the Orishas and the traditions and heritage of La Regla de Ocha [Santería] and La Regia Ifá [Ifá]." Fortunately, it offers a Spanish-language version of all the material.

Island of Salvation Botanica

2372 St. Claude Ave. #100, New Orleans, LA 70117

(504) 948-9961

islandofsalvationbotanica.com

This site is run by Mambo Sallie Ann Glassman, artist and author, and is the internet face for her physical botanica in New Orleans. It features handcrafted items created by Glassman, as well as candles, incense, oils, soaps, herbs, and even a shrine to Marie Laveau.

Enchantments

424 E. 9th St., New York, NY 10009

enchantmentsincnyc.com

This is the oldest continually run magick store in my hometown of NYC. It carries a wide array of candles, oils, and herbs useful for a variety of paths. It is one of my favorite places for incense and carved candles.

Hex New Orleans

1219 Decatur St., New Orleans, LA 70116

www.hexwitch.com

Christian Day and Brian Cain present a Witchcraft shop for those who still believe in magic and offer everything you need to cast your own spell: candles, incense, potions, jewelry, herbs, books, and voodoo dolls.

Crescent City Conjure

2402 Royal St., New Orleans, LA 70117

crescentcityconjure.us

This rising star of the Crescent City offers almost everything a practitioner could need.

Path of Awakenings

1212 N. Rampart St., New Orleans, LA 70116

crescentcityconjure.us

Fatima Mbodj creator of the New Orleans Oracle Deck also operates a wonderful store called Path of Awakenings.

Arts and Crafts: Botanica & Occult Shop

4901 Penn Ave., Pittsburgh, PA 15224

artsncraftspgh.com

With both a storefront and an online presence, this store offers a variety of supplies for those who follow Witchcraft, and also the ATRs. Founded by three knowledgeable practitioners with some serious style, I hope you check it out.

Buckland Museum of Witchcraft & Magick

2155 Broadview Rd., Cleveland, OH 44109

bucklandmuseum.org

I've spoken at events and universities all across the globe, but the Buckland Museum of Witchcraft and Magick was the first place to give me my own Voodoo exhibit. With archives, exhibits, and a wealth of knowledge, this museum is a must-see if you're in the area.

APPENDIX THREE
GLOSSARY OF TERMS

Adimu: Nonanimal offering.

Afonga (or Fonga): Popular West African rhythm and chant.

African Diaspora: The dispersal of African people, either voluntary or involuntary, throughout the world.

Aganyú: Father of Changó in Lucumí, owner of volcanoes.

Agwé: Vodou and Voodoo divinity seen as a patron of fisherpeople and boats.

Aida Wedo: Vodou and Voodoo creation goddess associated with a rainbow serpent.

Annie Christmas: Voodoo Lwa of the railroad.

Ashé/Ase/Axé (pronounced ah-shay): Life, grace, blood, kingship, growth, power, force, and energy, it has also recently been used in conversation to mean "so be it.".

Asiento: Initiation to become a Santera or Santero in Santería, literally "seated".

Asson: Ceremonial gourd rattle that is sometimes conferred as part of an initiation in Haitian Vodou.

Awo: Sacred knowledge, mystery.

Ayizan: Vodou Lwa of initiation.

Azaka (also known as Cousin): Vodou Lwa of agriculture and fieldworkers.

Babalawo: Ifá or Santería high priest.

Babaluaiye: Lucumí divinity for healing and smallpox.

Bamboula: Drum rhythm and dance popular in New Orleans and the Caribbean, it is said to have traveled with the enslaved Africans.

Banda: Voodoo rhythm and dance associated with the ancestors.

Barons Samedi and Cimetière: Embodiment of the named dead in Haitian Vodou.

Bembe: La Regla Lucumí drum ceremony.

Blanc Dani: Voodoo and Vodou creator Lwa associated with a white serpent.

Bossou: Vodou warlike divinity associated with the bull.

Botanica: Herbal supply store for purchasing ritual items.

Caboclos: Ancestor spirits worshipped in Brazil.

Candomblé: Variation of Brazilian African Traditional Religion.

Cascarilla: Powdered eggshell used for blessing and cleansing in Voodoo, Santería, and Ifá.

Centros: Brazilian centers of worship.

Changó: Lord of fire and the drum.

Congo/Kongo tribe: People originating from the Congo River area in West Africa.

Curanderos: Latin American healing priests and priestesses.

Damballa Wedo (pronounced way-do): Vodou serpent creator deity.

Diloggún: Divination with cowrie shells.

Ebo: Offering.

Egungun: Revered ancestor spirits in Ifá.

Elegguá/Eshú/Exú: Trickster god of the crossroads.

Elekes (also known as collares): Ritual initiation necklaces of Lucumí.

Erzulie/Ezili Freda: Vodou and Voodoo Lwa of love.

Gede: Vodou spirits of the dead.

Gede Nibo: Vodou ancestor spirit said to have a cinnamon anus and be very dapper.

Gran Bois: Vodou Lwa of the woods and of ganja.

Gris-gris (pronounced gree-gree): Voodoo or Hoodoo herbal spell mixture.

Hi John the Conqueror root: Species of Ipomoea plant used for court cases, luck, and success.

Hounfor: Vodou temple.

Houngan: Vodou priest.

Hounsi: Ritual assistant, literally "wife," in Vodou.

Iansa/Yansa: Orïsa/Orixa of the cemetery in the Ifá and Candomblé traditions, respectively.

Ibeji: Divine twins of the Yoruba pantheon.

Ibo people/Igbo people: Tribal group of people originating from West Africa, many were relocated as enslaved people to the South Carolina coast.

Ibo Point: The place in South Carolina where the Ibo were said to fly back to Africa.

Iemanja: Candomblé Orixa of the ocean.

Ifá: Practices of traditional Yoruba religion.

Ifá: Yoruba deity of divination.

Ile: Ifá or Lucumí spiritual house or temple.

Iya: Mother, used as a term of respect for priestesses.

Kabala: Ancient Jewish mystical teachings.

La Baleen: Vodou Lwa of whales, associated with LaSirene.

LaLune, Madame: Voodoo Lwa of the moon.

LaSirene: Vodou Lwa of the sea, often associated with LaBaleen.

Lavé Tet: Vodou water baptism.

Laveau, Marie: One of the great queens of New Orleans Voodoo.

Lebat, Papa: Crossroads deity of New Orleans Voodoo, similar to Legba.

Legba: Vodou and Voodoo Loa representing the paternal force of creation in the cosmos.

Louverture, Toussaint: One of the leaders of the Haitian revolution of 1804.

Lucumí: Afro-Cuban word for the practices derived from the Yoruba people of West Africa.

Lwa/Loa: Gods or goddess in Vodou.

Maman: The main ritual drum in Vodou.

Maman Brigitte: Vodou divinity of justice, wife of Baron Samedi, the first woman buried in every cemetery.

Mambo: Vodou priestess.

Mami Wata/Mami Water: Vodou, Voodoo, and Yoruba ancient water deity.

Marassa: Divine twins of the Vodou pantheon.

Maroons: enslaved Africans who found their way to freedom and lived in secluded areas. They were present in the Americas and the Caribbean. In Louisiana they inhabited the Bas de Fleuve region. Very often they were aided by indigenous individuals in the area.

Masa LaFlambeau: Vodou deity of purifying fire.

Myalism: Term given to Obeah practices in Jamaica and Belize that involve dancing, drumming, and trance-possession.

Nana Buluku: Yoruba and Lucumí maternal deity representing female courage, grand knowledge, and power.

Nanchons: Groups of Vodou Lwa that are seen as belonging to the same original tribal lineage.

Obá: Santería Orisha who resides in lakes. She is one of Changó's three wives.

Obatalá: Santería and Ifá androgynous Orisha of the clouds.

Obeah: Form of African Traditional Religion popular in Belize and Jamaica.

Ochosi/Oxossi/Osossi: Orisha of the hunt.

Oduduwa: Yoruban female creator deity.

Ogou/Ogún: Orisha and also Lwa of iron, war, technology.

Olodumare: Yoruba and Lucumí creator deity associated with the rainbow.

Olodus: Disciples who assist Orunmilá.

Olokun: Orisha of the depths of the ocean in Lucumí and Yoruba theology.

Olodumare/Olofin): Santería supreme creator deity represented by a dove.

Omiero: Herbal preparation or wash.

Omolu (also known as Babaluaiye/Sumbu): La Regla Lucumí Orisha of sickness, healing, and infectious disease; similar to the Yoruba Sonponno.

Opele chain: Eight halved nuts from the opele tree attached by a chain and used for divination in Ifá.

Orisha/Orïsa/Orixa: Name for the divine beings in Lucumí, Ifá, and Candomblé.

Orunla (also known as Orunmilá/Ifá): Orisha associated with divination.

Orunmilá (pronounced awroonmeela): Orisha of divination, also known as Ifá.

Osanyin (also known as Osain/Ossain/Aroni): Lucumí Orisha who rules herbal medicines.

Oshún : Orisha of love, beauty, dance, and more.

Ossain: see Osanyin.

Osun river: Nigerian river sacred to Osun (Oshún), the Orïsa of love, beauty, dance, and more.

Ouroboros: Mythological serpent depicted devouring its own tail.

Oxala: Orisha of peace and sky.

Oxumare: Candomblé Orixa represented by the rainbow serpent.

Oyá (pronounced oi yah): Orisha of lightning, the tornado, and the dead.

Paket Congo/Kongo: Magickal spell bundles of Vodou.

Palero/Palera: Priest or Priestess of the Palo Monte religion.

Palo: see Palo Monte.

Palo Monte (also known as Palo Mayombe/Palo): African Religious Tradition with a concentration on connection to the dead.

Pataki (pronounced pah-tak-ee): Lucumí myth.

Petit (Boulah): Smallest of the three ritual drums of Vodou.

Petro: Vodou nanchon characterized by heat and fire.

Pomba Gira (also known as Bomba Gira): Wife of Exú in Candomblé and Umbanda, known for her highly sexualized behavior.

Poteau Mitan: Center pole in Haitian Vodou.

Pretos Velhos: Spirits of honored enslaved people in Candomblé.

Rada: One of the Vodou nanchons believed to have come from the Arada region of West Africa.

Regla de Ocha: Alternate term for the practices of Lucumí, roughly translates in Spanish to "rule of the divine".

Rogación: La Regla Lucumí baptism ceremony.

Sanite Dede: One of the earliest recorded Voodoo priestesses in New Orleans.

Santería: Afro-Caribbean religious practices originating in Cuba and Puerto Rico. This is more correctly called La Regla Lucumí.

Santero/Santera: Initiated Priest/Priestess in Lucumí.

Segunda: Second ritual drum in Vodou.

Shilibo: Vodou and Voodoo Lwa of pure and shining joy.

Simbi: Serpent Lwa in Vodou, representative of magick and intelligence.

Sonponno (also known as Sakpata): see Babaluaiye.

Spirit Marriage: Sacred union between a Lwa and a Vodou practitioner.

Spiritism: Name of the religion revealed by Allen Kardec, which includes a belief in spirits and reincarnation.

Tambor: Santería drum ceremony.

Tarot: Ancient system of card-based divination originating in Italy.

Terrerio: Center of Candomblé religious practices. Used for rituals and housing sacred items.

Thunderstones: Special ritual stones for the Orisha Changó that are believed to have been struck by lightning.

Ti Malice: Vodou ancestor spirit.

Umbanda: Brazilian religion using elements of African, Buddhist, Hindu, and indigenous Amazonian sacred practices.

Vodou: (pronounced voh dew): Haitian form of the religion, translates literally as "spirit" or "deity".

Voodoo: The religion as practiced in New Orleans.

Voodoo Spiritual Temple: Authentic Voodoo temple in New Orleans, founded by Priestess Miriam Chamani and Priest Oswan Chamani in 1990.

Vévé: Ritual ground drawing for the Lwa often created in cornmeal, flour, or coffee.

Xango/Xangó: Candomblé god of fire.

Yanvalou: Sacred dance performed in Vodou and Voodoo.

Yemonja: (also known as Yemaya/Yemoja): Yoruban and Santería Orisha of the sea

INDEX

Aba Lofa (Elofa): 90-91
Abebe: 19
Aflakete: 14
Afonga: 21, 190
Aganyú: 77, 85, 190
Agwé: 28, 33-38, 190
Aida Wedo: 29-30, 46, 51, 54, 121, 190
AIDS: 19, 79
Aireelay: 90-91
Akanji, Adebisi: 111
Alafia: 21
Allspice: 96, 126
Almond tree: 48
Altars: (SEE: Shrines)
Amado, Jorge: 115, 143, 179, 182
Ambrose, Saint: 79
Amulet of Ogum (movie): 141
Anaïs: 29
Anansi: 95-96
Ancestor shrine: 117-118
Ancestor Worship
 — in Trinidad and Belize: 94
 — in Vodou: 34-35
 — in Voodoo and Hoodoo: 55
Angel Heart (movie): 144
Animal Magnetism: 127
Animal sacrifice: 10, 89, 170
Animal sacrifices: 89
Anise (anis): 108
Anne, Saint: 29, 60
Annie Christmas: 52, 190
Anthony, Saint: 59, 71, 102, 116
Arguments (arguing), with your spiritual elders/: 6
Armstrong, Louis: 51, 62
Art
 — of Trinidad and Belize: 94
 — of Vodou: 38-41
 — of Voodoo and Hoodoo: 61
 — of Yoruba (Ifá): 20

Ashé (ase; axé): 1-2, 5, 11-12, 15-21, 40-45, 55, 63-65, 71-77, 81, 89, 99, 108, 115, 134, 137, 190
Ashé Changó: 76
Asiento (kariocha): 83, 190
Assentamentos: 116
Asson: 31, 45, 190
Avocado: 48
Ayizan: 31, 48, 53, 171, 190
Azaka (Cousin)/: 31-32, 190

Babalawo: 7, 83, 190
Babaluaiye (Omolu; Sumbu; Sonponno): 13, 19, 79, 85-86, 103, 190, 194-196
Bamboula: 44, 51, 134, 191
Banana: 44, 48, 108
Banda: 43, 191
Barbara Africana: 77
Barbara, Saint: 77
Barons: 34, 43, 56, 191
Baron Samedi: 34-35, 38, 140-142, 193
Barra, Pierrot: 112, 175
Basil: 28, 66, 78, 87, 120, 124-128, 156, 160, 163-165
Bata: 80
Baths (bathing): 46, 77, 83, 119-120, 126, 135, 158, 179
Bay laurel: 47
Bay leaves: 163-164
Bean sprouts: 96
Believers, The (movie): 145
Bembe: 4, 80, 191
Ben-Aime, Gabriel: 41
Beretto, Sebastian: 98
Bibliomancy: 58
Birch Gum tree: 48
Bitter kola: 16, 23, 108
Black Doll Project: 166
Black Hawk: 64

Black Lives Matter: 167
Black pepper: 35, 162-163
Black pigs: 29
Blanc Dani: 32-33, 191
Blues Brothers 2000 (movie): 149
Bodies of Water: Voodoo Identity and Transformation (movie)/: 151
Bomba Gira (Pomba Gira): 100-102, 115-116, 195
Books, recommended: 173
Bossou: 32, 191
Botanicals (herbs) (SEE ALSO: specific botanicals)
— Candomblé, Umbanda, Quimbanda: 108
— Obeah: 96-97
— Santería: 87
— Vodou: 47-48
— Voodoo and Hoodoo: 66-67
— Yoruba (Ifá): 23
Botanicas: 59, 75, 186-187
Bottle trees: 94
Brazil
— botanicals of: 108
— calendar of: 107
— Candomblé in: 98-101
— music and dance: 106
— myths of: 107
— recommended books: 182-183
— shrines in: 115-117
— Spiritism in: 103-104
— Umbanda in: 105-106
Brick Dust: 38, 57, 159
Brother Dead: 95

Caboclos: 106, 191
Calabash gourd: 47
Calendar (feast days)
— Brazil: 107
— Santería: 85-86
— Shangó and Obeah: 94-95
— Vodou: 46
— Voodoo and Hoodoo: 64-65
— Yoruba (Ifá): 21
Camphor: 66, 159-160

Candle Spells: 123
Candomblé
— Botanicals: 108
— calendar: 107
— music and dance: 106
— myths of: 107
— Orixa: 100-103
— recommended books: 182-183
— shrines of: 115-117
Cashews: 76, 108
Catholic saints: (SEE: specific saints)
Chamani, Miriam: 184, 187, 197
Chamani, Oswan: 55, 92, 197
Chamba: 71
Chamomile: 88
Changó (Shangó; Jakuta): 10-11, 60, 65, 75-82, 85-91, 94-97, 110, 114, 132, 136, 171, 184-186, 190-191, 194-196
Charity: 8, 104, 122
Charles, Ray: 62-63
Chicory: 66
Christopher, Saint: 77
Church of Lukumí Babalu Aye vs. City of Hialeah (1993): 89
Cigar plant: 96
Cinnamon: 35, 76, 96, 120, 126, 158, 192
City of God (movie): 150
Cleanliness: 6, 13, 28, 73, 76, 114, 119
Cloves: 97, 163-165
Cocoa butter: 88
Coconut: 23, 71, 81, 84, 88, 115, 120, 123, 126-127, 135, 165
Columbus, Christopher: 26
Compassion: 8
Computer and Electronic Help Candle: 124
Congo: 27, 39, 43-45, 51, 62, 84, 90, 104, 191, 195
Copal: 66, 126
Cornmeal: 38, 48, 54, 137, 197
Cosentino, Donald J., Sacred Arts of Haitian Vodou/: 111
Cotton: 35, 47, 73, 120, 126,

155-156, 160
Council of Elders: 91, 97
Cowrie shells: 12, 84, 191
Creating a Magickal Journal: 136
Cypress: 66, 127

Da Logee: 92, 95
Da Lua: 92, 95
Damballa: 28-30, 33, 38, 43, 46-47, 51-54, 121, 191
Dance (dancing) (SEE ALSO: Drums)
— Afro-Brazilian: 106
— Santería: 80
— Vodou: 41
— Yoruba (Ifá): 20
Daughters of the Dust (movie)/: 138, 146-147
Deren, Maya: 34, 42, 140
Despojo: 81
Devil: 62, 70, 98-100, 115, 149
Dill weed: 160
Diloggún: 84, 191
Divination
— in magickal workings: 129
— in New Orleans Voodoo: 61
— in Santería: 83
Divination Oil: 128
Divine Horseman: The Living Gods of Haiti (movie): 140
Divine justice, gris-gris bag for: 126
Dolls, Voodoo: 6, 125, 188
Dona Flor and Her Two Husbands (movie): 143
Dracena fragrans: 108
Drapo: 41
Drums (drumming)
— Afro-Brazilian: 106
— recommended recordings: 183
— Santería: 80
— Vodou: 41
— Voodoo and Hoodoo: 61
— Yoruba (Ifá): 20
Dunham, Katherine: 42, 140, 152
Duppies: 93-94
Duvalier, Francois "Papa Doc": 38

Dymphna, Saint: 60, 64, 161

Ebejee: 92-94
Egungun, the: 18, 191
Elegguá (Elegua; Eshú): 13-15, 20-24, 52, 70-71, 75, 81-82, 85, 90, 115, 123, 133, 136, 146, 191
— Crossroads Bath to Create Opportunities: 120
— Elegguá Road Opener Candle: 123
Elekes: 69, 81-82, 191
Elofa (Aba Lofa): 90-91
Erzulie (Ezili): 28-29, 33, 37, 42, 46, 55, 61, 122, 177, 191
Esango (Sango): 13-16, 20
Eshú: 13-15, 20-24, 70-71, 90, 115, 133, 191
Eucalyptus: 88, 126
Exorcist, The (movie)/: 7
Expedite, Saint: 59
Exú: 100-102, 108, 115-116, 191, 195

Feast days: (SEE: Calendar)
Feast of the Yam: 44
Fictive kin: 2
Fig: 66
Films: 108, 138, 141-143, 149, 152
Five-finger grass: 66, 156
Flags: 41, 114, 133, 177
Francis, Saint: 74, 91
Frangipani: 88
Frankincense: 66, 158-160
Freda Dahomey: 55

Galangal root: 154-155
Gandolfo, Charles: 61
Ganja Bois (Gran Bois): 30-31, 46, 177, 192
Gardenia oil: 161
Gbadamosi, Buraimoh: 111
Gede spirits: 35
Gender roles: 9-10
George, Saint: 116
Geranium: 66

Get a Job Oil: 128
Ginger: 88, 96
Glassman, Sallie Ann: 53, 61, 179, 188
Glossary of Terms: 190
Grains of paradise: 160
Gran Bois (Ganga Bois): 30-31, 46, 177, 192
Gran Brigitte: 35
Gran Ibo: 31-32
Grave markers: 113
Green Pastures, The (movie): 139
Gris-gris bags: 125-126
Group Rituals: 131, 135
— Private Group Ritual: 134
— Public Group Ritual: 133
Guava: 96
Gu (gubasa): 17
Guinea pepper: 160-162

Haitian Vodou: (SEE: Vodou)
Happiness and Success Oil: 128
Harding, Rachel E.: 98, 183
Haskins, Jim: 178
Healing Oil: 128
Health, gris-gris bag for: 126
Heliotrope: 128
Hemp seed: 96, 126
Herbs: (SEE: Botanicals and specific herbs)
Hermes: 101
Hi John the Conqueror root: 57-58, 66, 120, 149, 156, 192
Holy water: 73, 117, 135, 149, 154-155, 160-161
Homeless, in New Orleans: 63
Hoodoo: 56-58
— botanicals: 66-67
— calendar: 64-65
— magickal items: 63-64
— magickal workings: 57-58
— music of: 61-63
— myths of: 65
— recommended books: 178-179
— saints associated with: 58-60
Hurston, Zora Neale: 42, 56, 72, 94, 147, 152-153, 156, 171, 177
Hyssop: 66, 156-157

Iansa: (SEE: Oyá)
Ibeji (Ibbeyi): 19, 79, 86, 107, 117, 192
Ibo spirits: 27, 32
Iemanja: 103, 107-109, 117, 192
Ifá: 5-7, 12, 16, 20-21, 74, 83, 87, 103, 110-111, 119, 133, 173, 185-187, 190-194
Ilekes: 81
Initiations: 2-5, 26, 31, 45, 48, 83, 119, 190
— Santería: 81, 181
Inle: 80
Irukere: 64, 73
Isidore, Saint: 32
Itotele: 80
Iya: 80, 192

Jacques, Saint: 36
Jakuta: (SEE: Changó)
Jalop: 66
Jasmine: 28, 66, 120, 161
Jazz music: 61-62, 201
Jesus Christ: 58-60, 104
Job Oil, Get a: 128
John, Saint: 46, 65-67, 79, 122
Johnson, Robert: 62
Jonah, Saint: 91
Jude, Saint: 92, 95
Justice, gris-gris bag for: 126

Kardec, Allan: 103
Kariocha (asiento): 83, 190
King Solomon Oil: 128
Krishna: 19
Kumina: 93

LaSirene: 33, 36, 53, 192-193
Laveau, Marie: 49, 62, 113, 122, 134-135, 156, 163, 172, 188, 193
Lavender: 66, 120, 124-128, 158
Lavé Tet: 26, 37, 132, 193

Lebat, Papa: 52, 62, 133
Legacy of the Spirits (movie): 143
Legba: 3, 27-28, 31, 39, 45, 52, 62, 121, 133-137, 146, 177, 184, 193
Lemon: 66, 96, 124-129, 161-162
Lemon balm: 66
Lemon verbena: 66, 129
Les Barons: 34
Les Gede: 34
Lime: 96, 126-127
Lineages: 2, 26, 186
Listening: 6
Littaud, Georges: 41
Live and Let Die (movie): 140-141, 145
Lodestone: 66, 88, 149
Love Bath: 120
Love, gris-gris bag for: 126
Lusty encounters, gris-gris bag for: 126
Lwa (SEE ALSO: Specific Spirits): 5-10, 25-33, 36-47, 51-58, 62-64, 110-112, 121-122, 131-137, 169, 176-178, 184, 187, 190-197
— Vodou: 26-36
— Voodoo: 52-56

Madame LaLune: 54
Madame Satan (movie): 138-139
Magic flower: 96
Magickal items: 45, 63, 71, 99, 187
Magickal Items
— Vodou: 45
— Voodoo and Hoodoo: 63-64
Magickal oils: 126
Magickal workings
— for protection and protest: 154
— gris-gris bags: 125
— recipes for revolution: 162-165
— ritual cleansing and baths: 119
— to remove unwanted influences: 120
— véve magic: 121
— Voodoo dolls: 125
— with candles: 123

Mama Latay: 90-91
Maman Brigitte: 34-35, 43, 47, 56, 112-113, 121, 132, 166, 193
Mambo: 7, 26, 31, 37, 42, 45, 53, 61, 112, 121-122, 130-131, 178, 183, 188, 193
Mami Wata: 13, 19, 53, 152, 193
Mami Water: 53, 193
Marassa: 30, 46-47, 53, 178, 193
Mardi Gras: 59, 63-64
Mardi Gras Indians: 59, 63-64
Maria Mulambo: 100-101
Maria Padilla: 100-101
Marley, Bob: 94
Maroon: 63
Marriage, gris-gris bag for: 126
Marriage, Spirit/: 36-37, 196
Marta, Saint: 60, 77-78
Martin DePorres, Saint: 60
Martinié, Louis: 51-52, 61, 184
Mary Magdalene: 60
Masa: 33, 193
Masks, Voodoo: 63
Metalwork: 38
Michael, Saint: 85
Midnight in the Garden of Good and Evil (movie): 147
Miel para Oshún (movie): 150
Millet: 23
Mint: 79, 108
Mombin: 48
Money, drawing: 57-58
Money Oil: 129
Montanee, John (Dr. John): 57, 187
Moses: 28-29, 88, 152
Moses in the Cradle: 88
Movies: 138
Music (SEE ALSO: Dance)
— Afro-Brazilian: 106
— Santería: 80
— Vodou: 41
— Voodoo and Hoodoo: 61
— Yoruba (Ifá): 20
Myalism (Myal): 93, 97
Myrrh: 66, 127, 154-160

Myrtle: 66
Myths (mythology)
— Afro-Brazilian: 107
— Jamaican: 95
— Santería: 86
— Vodou: 46
— Voodoo and Hoodoo: 65
— Yoruba (Ifá): 22

Nana Buluku (Nana Buukun): 19, 79, 103, 194
Nema: 61
New Orleans Voodoo and Hoodoo: (SEE: Hoodoo; Voodoo)
New Orleans Voodoo Museum: 55, 178
Nia and Umoja (Purpose and Unity in the Community): 165-167
Nigeria: 3, 13, 16-18, 24, 69, 75, 117-119, 173
Nla: 23
Nutmeg: 35, 57, 76, 96, 128-129

Obá: 12, 77-79, 86, 143, 194
Obatalá: 13, 64, 73-76, 82, 85-88, 111, 147, 194
Obeah: 10, 90-97, 110, 127, 193-194
— botanicals of: 96-97
— calendar: 94-95
— future direction of: 97
— traditions in: 92-94
Obeah Oil: 127
Ochosi (Oxossi; Osossi): 17, 71-73, 81-82, 86-87, 103, 107-108, 116, 123, 194
— candle spell for: 123
Ogou: 12-13, 17, 20, 28, 33, 36-38, 45, 52, 122, 134, 177, 194
Ogum: 102, 106-108, 116, 141
Ogun: 17, 36, 46, 90-91, 173, 184
Oils: 126
Okonkolo: 80
Olive oil: 23, 29, 67, 127-128, 165
Olodumare (Olorun; Olofin): 12-13, 23, 69, 194

Olokun: 13, 18-19, 75, 194
Omela: 91
Omolu (Babaluaiye; Sumbu): 13, 19, 79, 85-86, 103, 190, 194-196
Onion: 23, 162-165
Orchid: 97
Orïsa (Orisha; Orixa) (SEE ALSO: Specific Spirits): 1, 6-23, 51, 60, 64, 69-91, 94, 98-111, 114-117, 123-124, 131-137, 142, 146, 150, 153, 169-174, 178-182, 185-187, 192-197, 201
— Candomblé: 100-103
— in Trinidad: 90-92
— Santería: 69-80
— Yoruba (Ifá): 12-20
Orunmilá (Orunla; Ifá): 12-16, 23, 74, 82, 86, 194
Osanyin (Osonyin; Osain): 79-82, 85, 90-91, 195
Oshún: 4, 55, 74-79, 82-85, 89-90, 114, 132-134, 150, 179, 195
Oshun-African Magickal Quarterly: 201
Ossain: (SEE: Osanyin)
Osun river: 16, 75, 195
Oxala: 103, 195
Oxossi: (SEE: Ochosi)
Oxum: 102-103, 107, 117
Oxumare: 107, 117, 195

Paket Congo: 45, 195
Palm oil: 17, 23, 39, 108, 128, 135
Palo Mayombe: 1, 84-85, 171, 195
Palo Monte: 84-85, 104, 180, 195
Papa Lebat: 52, 62, 133
Papa Legba (SEE ALSO: Elegguá; Papa Lebat): 27, 31, 121, 135-137, 177, 184
Papa Loko (Loco Attisou): 31, 54
Papaya: 108
Parsley: 88, 120, 163-165
Pataki: 195
Patchouli: 67, 76, 126, 136, 158
Patrick, Saint: 29

Paul, Saint: 60
Peji: 116
Peter, Saint: 28, 59, 71, 85, 92-94
Petro spirits: 27-29, 44, 195
Pimento: 96
Pine: 76, 88, 126
Pinto, Louisa: 98
Pocomania: 93
Polytheism: 9
Pomba Gira (Bomba Gira): 100-102, 115-116, 195
Possession: 7-8, 19, 29-31, 44, 58, 71-72, 93, 100-102, 106, 170, 176, 180, 183-185
Poteau mitan: 25, 133, 195
Pretos Velhos: 106, 116, 195
Primero Congresso de Espiritismo de Umbanda (1941): 105
Private group rituals: 134
Protection, gris-gris bag for: 125
Protection Oil: 126-127
Protest magick: 154
Psychic Power Bath: 120
Public group rituals: 133
Pumpkin seeds: 23

Quimbanda: 98, 104-105, 108, 115

Rada spirits: 27-28, 195
Raphael (Rafael), Saint: 80, 91, 94
Raymond, Saint: 59
Readings, recommended: 173
Recipes for Revolution: 162-165
Recordings, recommended: 183
Regla de Ocha: (SEE: Santería)
Reincarnation: 103-104, 196
Rita, Saint: 59-60, 78
Ritual Feasts: 122
Rituals: 1, 4, 8-10, 15-20, 25-27, 31-46, 49-52, 55, 58, 62-64, 69-84, 89-93, 99-102, 105-107, 110-119, 122, 130-137, 140-145, 152, 160, 164, 170, 175-184, 191-197, 201
— cleansing for: 119
— group: 131

— solitary: 135
Rogación: 81, 147, 196
Root magick: 153-154
Rosemary: 88, 123-124, 156, 163
Rose of Jericho Oil: 128
Rue: 88, 108

Sacred art: (SEE: Art)
Sacrifice: 10, 17, 21, 72, 83-84, 89, 98, 103, 116, 140-141, 145, 157, 169-170
Sacrifices: 14, 70, 89, 99, 157-158
Saints: (SEE: specific saints)
Sakpata: (SEE: Babaluaiye)
Samba de Teste: 106
Sango (Esango): 13-16, 20
Sanite Dede: 196
Sansevieria Snake Plant: 96
Santería: 1-10, 15, 55, 69-71, 79-81, 85-89, 92, 104, 110, 113-114, 133, 138, 145, 169-171, 174, 180-182, 187, 190-191, 194-197, 201
— botanicals: 87
— calendar: 85-86
— divination: 83
— divine legends of: 86
— drumming and dance: 80
— initiations: 81, 181
— Orisha: 69-80
— Palo Monte or Palo Mayombe: 84
— persecution and prosecution: 88
— recommended books: 180
— religious rituals: 130
— shrines of: 113
Sarabanda: 85
Sassafras: 67
Sea salt: 124-126, 159, 164
Self-Initiation: 5
Seminole Indians: 72-73
Sensitive plant: 108
Sequin flag: 41
Sesame seed: 125-126
Sesame seeds: 67
Sete Encruzilhadas: 100
Shangó: 90

— calendar: 94-95
— future direction of: 97
— recommended books: 180
Shea butter: 13, 23
Shrines (altars): 110
— creating ancestor: 117
— in Brazil: 115
— in Trinidad: 114
— of Santería: 113
— of Vodou: 111
— of Voodoo: 112
— of Yoruba (Ifá): 111
Simbi: 33-34, 51, 196
Simon, Saint: 92, 95
Slaves and slavery: 10, 26-27, 38, 43, 49-51, 69, 90, 99, 106-107, 146
Solitary rituals: 135
Something Wild (movie)/: 143
Sonponno (Sakpata; Babaluaiye): 13, 19, 79, 85-86, 190, 194-196
Spanish moss: 67, 125
Spearmint: 67, 88, 124, 159-160
Spiritism: 103-104
Spirit Marriage: 36-37, 196
Spiritual Cleansing Oil: 127
Spiritual teacher, finding a: 2, 123
Stormy Weather: 44, 140
Stormy Weather (movie): 44, 140
Success, gris-gris bag for: 126
Success Oil: 128
Sugar Hill (movie): 141-142
Sumbu (Babaluaiye; Omolu): 13, 19, 79, 85-86, 103, 190, 194-196

Taboos: 8-10, 76, 82, 169
Tambor: 80, 196
Temple flags: 114
Theresa, Saint: 77-78
Thompson, Robert Farris, Flash of the Spirit: 20, 175
Throwing the shells: 84
Thunderstones: 16, 76, 117, 196
Ti Malice: 34-35, 196
Tobacco: 48, 64, 123
Training: 2, 5-6, 48, 89, 169, 201

Trance: 19, 31
Travel, gris-gris bag for: 125
Trees, bottle: 94
Trinidad, Shangó and Orisha: (SEE: Shangó)
Tronas: 114

Ulrich, Saint: 35
Umbanda: 98, 104-110, 115-116, 141-143, 182, 195-196

Varig Airlines: 99
Vévés: 25, 33-35, 38-42, 48-50, 53-56, 61-63, 112-113, 121-122, 133, 136-137, 171, 177-180, 197
Vincent de Paul, Saint: 32
Violet: 88, 156
Virgin of Caridad del Cobre: 76, 88
Vodou: 1, 4-9, 25-27, 30-48, 110-114, 117-121, 125, 130-133, 140-143, 147, 151, 165, 171, 175-178, 184, 190-197
— art of: 38-41
— botanicals: 47-48
— calendar: 46
— drumming and dance: 41
— Feast of the Yam: 44
— future direction of: 48
— in the ancestors and: 34-35
— magickal items: 45
— myths of: 46
— origins of: 26
— political history of: 38
— possession: 44
— recommended books: 175
— shrines of: 111
— spirit marriage and: 36
— the Lwa: 26-36
Voodoo: 9-10, 49-51, 58, 61-65, 110, 125, 130, 138-139, 142-147, 150-152, 169-171, 177-179, 184-187, 190-193, 197, 201
— art of: 61
— botanicals: 66-67
— calendar: 64-65

— divination: 61
— dolls: 125
— history of: 49-51
— magickal items: 63-64
— magickal workings: 57-58
— music of: 61
— myths of: 65
— recommended books: 178
— religious rituals: 137
— saints associated with: 58-60
— shrines of: 112
— the ancestors and: 55
— the Lwa: 52-56
Voodoo Dawn (movie): 145, 170
Voodoo Spiritual Temple (New Orleans): 51-55, 61, 68, 92, 133, 182-184, 187, 197

— sacred stories of: 22
— shrines of: 111
— the Orïsa: 12-20
— water offerings: 119

Zombies: 6, 50, 94, 141-142, 185

Warriors initiation: 82
Wenger, Susanne: 111
West Africa: (SEE: Yoruba (Ifá) religion)
White lilies: 97
Wormwood: 108

Xe do Caixão (movie): 142

Yam: 44-48
Yansa: (SEE: Oyá)
Yanvalou: 43, 107, 135, 184, 197
Yemonja (Yemaya; Yemanja): 12-13, 18-19, 74-75, 82, 85, 90-92, 109, 124, 181, 197
— Candle: 124
Yoruba (Ifá) religion: 5-7, 12-23, 27, 32, 53-55, 69-71, 74, 79, 83, 87, 91, 98, 103, 110-111, 119, 133, 148, 173-174, 179, 184-187, 190-194
— art of: 20
— botanicals: 23
— calendar: 21
— future direction of: 24
— music and dance of: 20
— recommended books: 173-175

ABOUT THE AUTHOR

Lilith Dorsey, MA, resides in New Orleans, a city known worldwide for Voodoo and Hoodoo. They have a rich background in Afro-Caribbean and Native American spirituality. Lilith edited and published the *Oshun-African Magickal Quarterly*, filmed and produced the documentary *Bodies of Water: Voodoo Identity and Tranceformation*, and co-hosted the YouTube show Witchcraft & Voodoo. They were also both choreographer and performer for jazz legend Dr. John's Night Tripper Voodoo Show. Their traditional education focused on plant science, anthropology, and film at the University of Rhode Island, New York University, and the University of London, and their magickal training includes numerous initiations into Santería—also known as Lucumí, Haitian Vodoun, and New Orleans Voodoo. They have been a professional psychic and teacher for over three decades and are a frequent presenter at festivals and gatherings, including HexFest, WitchCon, Sirius Rising, Witch'sFest USA, New York City Pagan Pride Day, and the Earth Warriors Festival. Lilith is the author of the bestselling *Orishas, Goddesses, and Voodoo Queens* (Weiser, 2020), *Water Magic* (Llewellyn Worldwide, 2020), and *The African-American Ritual Cookbook* (Kindle, 2012).

www.ingramcontent.com/pod-product-compliance
Lightning Source LLC
Chambersburg PA
CBHW060354080526
44583CB00012B/305